C-1879 CAREER EXAMINATION SERIES

This is your
PASSBOOK for...

Laboratory Assistant

Test Preparation Study Guide
Questions & Answers

COPYRIGHT NOTICE

This book is SOLELY intended for, is sold ONLY to, and its use is RESTRICTED to individual, bona fide applicants or candidates who qualify by virtue of having seriously filed applications for appropriate license, certificate, professional and/or promotional advancement, higher school matriculation, scholarship, or other legitimate requirements of education and/or governmental authorities.

This book is NOT intended for use, class instruction, tutoring, training, duplication, copying, reprinting, excerption, or adaptation, etc., by:

1) Other publishers
2) Proprietors and/or Instructors of "Coaching" and/or Preparatory Courses
3) Personnel and/or Training Divisions of commercial, industrial, and governmental organizations
4) Schools, colleges, or universities and/or their departments and staffs, including teachers and other personnel
5) Testing Agencies or Bureaus
6) Study groups which seek by the purchase of a single volume to copy and/or duplicate and/or adapt this material for use by the group as a whole without having purchased individual volumes for each of the members of the group
7) Et al.

Such persons would be in violation of appropriate Federal and State statutes.

PROVISION OF LICENSING AGREEMENTS – Recognized educational, commercial, industrial, and governmental institutions and organizations, and others legitimately engaged in educational pursuits, including training, testing, and measurement activities, may address request for a licensing agreement to the copyright owners, who will determine whether, and under what conditions, including fees and charges, the materials in this book may be used them. In other words, a licensing facility exists for the legitimate use of the material in this book on other than an individual basis. However, it is asseverated and affirmed here that the material in this book CANNOT be used without the receipt of the express permission of such a licensing agreement from the Publishers. Inquiries re licensing should be addressed to the company, attention rights and permissions department.

All rights reserved, including the right of reproduction in whole or in part, in any form or by any means, electronic or mechanical, including photocopying, recording, or by any information storage and retrieval system, without permission in writing from the Publisher.

Copyright © 2025 by

National Learning Corporation

212 Michael Drive, Syosset, NY 11791
(516) 921-8888 • www.passbooks.com
E-mail: info@passbooks.com

PASSBOOK® SERIES

THE *PASSBOOK® SERIES* has been created to prepare applicants and candidates for the ultimate academic battlefield – the examination room.

At some time in our lives, each and every one of us may be required to take an examination – for validation, matriculation, admission, qualification, registration, certification, or licensure.

Based on the assumption that every applicant or candidate has met the basic formal educational standards, has taken the required number of courses, and read the necessary texts, the *PASSBOOK® SERIES* furnishes the one special preparation which may assure passing with confidence, instead of failing with insecurity. Examination questions – together with answers – are furnished as the basic vehicle for study so that the mysteries of the examination and its compounding difficulties may be eliminated or diminished by a sure method.

This book is meant to help you pass your examination provided that you qualify and are serious in your objective.

The entire field is reviewed through the huge store of content information which is succinctly presented through a provocative and challenging approach – the question-and-answer method.

A climate of success is established by furnishing the correct answers at the end of each test.

You soon learn to recognize types of questions, forms of questions, and patterns of questioning. You may even begin to anticipate expected outcomes.

You perceive that many questions are repeated or adapted so that you can gain acute insights, which may enable you to score many sure points.

You learn how to confront new questions, or types of questions, and to attack them confidently and work out the correct answers.

You note objectives and emphases, and recognize pitfalls and dangers, so that you may make positive educational adjustments.

Moreover, you are kept fully informed in relation to new concepts, methods, practices, and directions in the field.

You discover that you are actually taking the examination all the time: you are preparing for the examination by "taking" an examination, not by reading extraneous and/or supererogatory textbooks.

In short, this PASSBOOK®, used directedly, should be an important factor in helping you to pass your test.

LABORATORY ASSISTANT

DUTIES
Supervises the cleaning of laboratory equipment or assists in routine laboratory tests; performs related duties as required.

SUBJECT OF EXAMINATION
Written test designed to test for knowledge, skills, and/or abilities in such areas as:
1. Laboratory principles and practices;
2. Laboratory equipment and glassware;
3. Arithmetic reasoning; and
4. Supervision.

HOW TO TAKE A TEST

I. YOU MUST PASS AN EXAMINATION

A. WHAT EVERY CANDIDATE SHOULD KNOW

Examination applicants often ask us for help in preparing for the written test. What can I study in advance? What kinds of questions will be asked? How will the test be given? How will the papers be graded?

As an applicant for a civil service examination, you may be wondering about some of these things. Our purpose here is to suggest effective methods of advance study and to describe civil service examinations.

Your chances for success on this examination can be increased if you know how to prepare. Those "pre-examination jitters" can be reduced if you know what to expect. You can even experience an adventure in good citizenship if you know why civil service exams are given.

B. WHY ARE CIVIL SERVICE EXAMINATIONS GIVEN?

Civil service examinations are important to you in two ways. As a citizen, you want public jobs filled by employees who know how to do their work. As a job seeker, you want a fair chance to compete for that job on an equal footing with other candidates. The best-known means of accomplishing this two-fold goal is the competitive examination.

Exams are widely publicized throughout the nation. They may be administered for jobs in federal, state, city, municipal, town or village governments or agencies.

Any citizen may apply, with some limitations, such as the age or residence of applicants. Your experience and education may be reviewed to see whether you meet the requirements for the particular examination. When these requirements exist, they are reasonable and applied consistently to all applicants. Thus, a competitive examination may cause you some uneasiness now, but it is your privilege and safeguard.

C. HOW ARE CIVIL SERVICE EXAMS DEVELOPED?

Examinations are carefully written by trained technicians who are specialists in the field known as "psychological measurement," in consultation with recognized authorities in the field of work that the test will cover. These experts recommend the subject matter areas or skills to be tested; only those knowledges or skills important to your success on the job are included. The most reliable books and source materials available are used as references. Together, the experts and technicians judge the difficulty level of the questions.

Test technicians know how to phrase questions so that the problem is clearly stated. Their ethics do not permit "trick" or "catch" questions. Questions may have been tried out on sample groups, or subjected to statistical analysis, to determine their usefulness.

Written tests are often used in combination with performance tests, ratings of training and experience, and oral interviews. All of these measures combine to form the best-known means of finding the right person for the right job.

II. HOW TO PASS THE WRITTEN TEST

A. NATURE OF THE EXAMINATION

To prepare intelligently for civil service examinations, you should know how they differ from school examinations you have taken. In school you were assigned certain definite pages to read or subjects to cover. The examination questions were quite detailed and usually emphasized memory. Civil service exams, on the other hand, try to discover your present ability to perform the duties of a position, plus your potentiality to learn these duties. In other words, a civil service exam attempts to predict how successful you will be. Questions cover such a broad area that they cannot be as minute and detailed as school exam questions.

In the public service similar kinds of work, or positions, are grouped together in one "class." This process is known as *position-classification*. All the positions in a class are paid according to the salary range for that class. One class title covers all of these positions, and they are all tested by the same examination.

B. FOUR BASIC STEPS

1) Study the announcement

How, then, can you know what subjects to study? Our best answer is: "Learn as much as possible about the class of positions for which you've applied." The exam will test the knowledge, skills and abilities needed to do the work.

Your most valuable source of information about the position you want is the official exam announcement. This announcement lists the training and experience qualifications. Check these standards and apply only if you come reasonably close to meeting them.

The brief description of the position in the examination announcement offers some clues to the subjects which will be tested. Think about the job itself. Review the duties in your mind. Can you perform them, or are there some in which you are rusty? Fill in the blank spots in your preparation.

Many jurisdictions preview the written test in the exam announcement by including a section called "Knowledge and Abilities Required," "Scope of the Examination," or some similar heading. Here you will find out specifically what fields will be tested.

2) Review your own background

Once you learn in general what the position is all about, and what you need to know to do the work, ask yourself which subjects you already know fairly well and which need improvement. You may wonder whether to concentrate on improving your strong areas or on building some background in your fields of weakness. When the announcement has specified "some knowledge" or "considerable knowledge," or has used adjectives like "beginning principles of…" or "advanced … methods," you can get a clue as to the number and difficulty of questions to be asked in any given field. More questions, and hence broader coverage, would be included for those subjects which are more important in the work. Now weigh your strengths and weaknesses against the job requirements and prepare accordingly.

3) Determine the level of the position

Another way to tell how intensively you should prepare is to understand the level of the job for which you are applying. Is it the entering level? In other words, is this the position in which beginners in a field of work are hired? Or is it an intermediate or advanced level? Sometimes this is indicated by such words as "Junior" or "Senior" in the class title. Other jurisdictions use Roman numerals to designate the level – Clerk I, Clerk II, for example. The word "Supervisor" sometimes appears in the title. If the level is not indicated by the title, check the description of duties. Will you be working under very close supervision, or will you have responsibility for independent decisions in this work?

4) Choose appropriate study materials

Now that you know the subjects to be examined and the relative amount of each subject to be covered, you can choose suitable study materials. For beginning level jobs, or even advanced ones, if you have a pronounced weakness in some aspect of your training, read a modern, standard textbook in that field. Be sure it is up to date and has general coverage. Such books are normally available at your library, and the librarian will be glad to help you locate one. For entry-level positions, questions of appropriate difficulty are chosen – neither highly advanced questions, nor those too simple. Such questions require careful thought but not advanced training.

If the position for which you are applying is technical or advanced, you will read more advanced, specialized material. If you are already familiar with the basic principles of your field, elementary textbooks would waste your time. Concentrate on advanced textbooks and technical periodicals. Think through the concepts and review difficult problems in your field.

These are all general sources. You can get more ideas on your own initiative, following these leads. For example, training manuals and publications of the government agency which employs workers in your field can be useful, particularly for technical and professional positions. A letter or visit to the government department involved may result in more specific study suggestions, and certainly will provide you with a more definite idea of the exact nature of the position you are seeking.

III. KINDS OF TESTS

Tests are used for purposes other than measuring knowledge and ability to perform specified duties. For some positions, it is equally important to test ability to make adjustments to new situations or to profit from training. In others, basic mental abilities not dependent on information are essential. Questions which test these things may not appear as pertinent to the duties of the position as those which test for knowledge and information. Yet they are often highly important parts of a fair examination. For very general questions, it is almost impossible to help you direct your study efforts. What we can do is to point out some of the more common of these general abilities needed in public service positions and describe some typical questions.

1) General information

Broad, general information has been found useful for predicting job success in some kinds of work. This is tested in a variety of ways, from vocabulary lists to questions about current events. Basic background in some field of work, such as sociology or economics, may be sampled in a group of questions. Often these are principles which have become familiar to most persons through exposure rather than through formal training. It is difficult to advise you how to study for these questions; being alert to the world around you is our best suggestion.

2) Verbal ability

An example of an ability needed in many positions is verbal or language ability. Verbal ability is, in brief, the ability to use and understand words. Vocabulary and grammar tests are typical measures of this ability. Reading comprehension or paragraph interpretation questions are common in many kinds of civil service tests. You are given a paragraph of written material and asked to find its central meaning.

3) Numerical ability

Number skills can be tested by the familiar arithmetic problem, by checking paired lists of numbers to see which are alike and which are different, or by interpreting charts and graphs. In the latter test, a graph may be printed in the test booklet which you are asked to use as the basis for answering questions.

4) Observation

A popular test for law-enforcement positions is the observation test. A picture is shown to you for several minutes, then taken away. Questions about the picture test your ability to observe both details and larger elements.

5) Following directions

In many positions in the public service, the employee must be able to carry out written instructions dependably and accurately. You may be given a chart with several columns, each column listing a variety of information. The questions require you to carry out directions involving the information given in the chart.

6) Skills and aptitudes

Performance tests effectively measure some manual skills and aptitudes. When the skill is one in which you are trained, such as typing or shorthand, you can practice. These tests are often very much like those given in business school or high school courses. For many of the other skills and aptitudes, however, no short-time preparation can be made. Skills and abilities natural to you or that you have developed throughout your lifetime are being tested.

Many of the general questions just described provide all the data needed to answer the questions and ask you to use your reasoning ability to find the answers. Your best preparation for these tests, as well as for tests of facts and ideas, is to be at your physical and mental best. You, no doubt, have your own methods of getting into an exam-taking mood and keeping "in shape." The next section lists some ideas on this subject.

IV. KINDS OF QUESTIONS

Only rarely is the "essay" question, which you answer in narrative form, used in civil service tests. Civil service tests are usually of the short-answer type. Full instructions for answering these questions will be given to you at the examination. But in case this is your first experience with short-answer questions and separate answer sheets, here is what you need to know:

1) Multiple-choice Questions

Most popular of the short-answer questions is the "multiple choice" or "best answer" question. It can be used, for example, to test for factual knowledge, ability to solve problems or judgment in meeting situations found at work.

A multiple-choice question is normally one of three types—

- It can begin with an incomplete statement followed by several possible endings. You are to find the one ending which *best* completes the statement, although some of the others may not be entirely wrong.
- It can also be a complete statement in the form of a question which is answered by choosing one of the statements listed.

- It can be in the form of a problem – again you select the best answer.

Here is an example of a multiple-choice question with a discussion which should give you some clues as to the method for choosing the right answer:

When an employee has a complaint about his assignment, the action which will *best* help him overcome his difficulty is to
   A. discuss his difficulty with his coworkers
   B. take the problem to the head of the organization
   C. take the problem to the person who gave him the assignment
   D. say nothing to anyone about his complaint

In answering this question, you should study each of the choices to find which is best. Consider choice "A" – Certainly an employee may discuss his complaint with fellow employees, but no change or improvement can result, and the complaint remains unresolved. Choice "B" is a poor choice since the head of the organization probably does not know what assignment you have been given, and taking your problem to him is known as "going over the head" of the supervisor. The supervisor, or person who made the assignment, is the person who can clarify it or correct any injustice. Choice "C" is, therefore, correct. To say nothing, as in choice "D," is unwise. Supervisors have and interest in knowing the problems employees are facing, and the employee is seeking a solution to his problem.

2) True/False Questions

The "true/false" or "right/wrong" form of question is sometimes used. Here a complete statement is given. Your job is to decide whether the statement is right or wrong.

SAMPLE: A roaming cell-phone call to a nearby city costs less than a non-roaming call to a distant city.

This statement is wrong, or false, since roaming calls are more expensive.

This is not a complete list of all possible question forms, although most of the others are variations of these common types. You will always get complete directions for answering questions. Be sure you understand *how* to mark your answers – ask questions until you do.

V. RECORDING YOUR ANSWERS

Computer terminals are used more and more today for many different kinds of exams.
For an examination with very few applicants, you may be told to record your answers in the test booklet itself. Separate answer sheets are much more common. If this separate answer sheet is to be scored by machine – and this is often the case – it is highly important that you mark your answers correctly in order to get credit.

An electronic scoring machine is often used in civil service offices because of the speed with which papers can be scored. Machine-scored answer sheets must be marked with a pencil, which will be given to you. This pencil has a high graphite content which responds to the electronic scoring machine. As a matter of fact, stray dots may register as answers, so do not let your pencil rest on the answer sheet while you are pondering the correct answer. Also, if your pencil lead breaks or is otherwise defective, ask for another.

Since the answer sheet will be dropped in a slot in the scoring machine, be careful not to bend the corners or get the paper crumpled.

The answer sheet normally has five vertical columns of numbers, with 30 numbers to a column. These numbers correspond to the question numbers in your test booklet. After each number, going across the page are four or five pairs of dotted lines. These short dotted lines have small letters or numbers above them. The first two pairs may also have a "T" or "F" above the letters. This indicates that the first two pairs only are to be used if the questions are of the true-false type. If the questions are multiple choice, disregard the "T" and "F" and pay attention only to the small letters or numbers.

Answer your questions in the manner of the sample that follows:

32. The largest city in the United States is
    A. Washington, D.C.
    B. New York City
    C. Chicago
    D. Detroit
    E. San Francisco

1) Choose the answer you think is best. (New York City is the largest, so "B" is correct.)
2) Find the row of dotted lines numbered the same as the question you are answering. (Find row number 32)
3) Find the pair of dotted lines corresponding to the answer. (Find the pair of lines under the mark "B.")
4) Make a solid black mark between the dotted lines.

VI. BEFORE THE TEST

Common sense will help you find procedures to follow to get ready for an examination. Too many of us, however, overlook these sensible measures. Indeed, nervousness and fatigue have been found to be the most serious reasons why applicants fail to do their best on civil service tests. Here is a list of reminders:

- Begin your preparation early – Don't wait until the last minute to go scurrying around for books and materials or to find out what the position is all about.
- Prepare continuously – An hour a night for a week is better than an all-night cram session. This has been definitely established. What is more, a night a week for a month will return better dividends than crowding your study into a shorter period of time.
- Locate the place of the exam – You have been sent a notice telling you when and where to report for the examination. If the location is in a different town or otherwise unfamiliar to you, it would be well to inquire the best route and learn something about the building.
- Relax the night before the test – Allow your mind to rest. Do not study at all that night. Plan some mild recreation or diversion; then go to bed early and get a good night's sleep.
- Get up early enough to make a leisurely trip to the place for the test – This way unforeseen events, traffic snarls, unfamiliar buildings, etc. will not upset you.
- Dress comfortably – A written test is not a fashion show. You will be known by number and not by name, so wear something comfortable.

- Leave excess paraphernalia at home – Shopping bags and odd bundles will get in your way. You need bring only the items mentioned in the official notice you received; usually everything you need is provided. Do not bring reference books to the exam. They will only confuse those last minutes and be taken away from you when in the test room.
- Arrive somewhat ahead of time – If because of transportation schedules you must get there very early, bring a newspaper or magazine to take your mind off yourself while waiting.
- Locate the examination room – When you have found the proper room, you will be directed to the seat or part of the room where you will sit. Sometimes you are given a sheet of instructions to read while you are waiting. Do not fill out any forms until you are told to do so; just read them and be prepared.
- Relax and prepare to listen to the instructions
- If you have any physical problem that may keep you from doing your best, be sure to tell the test administrator. If you are sick or in poor health, you really cannot do your best on the exam. You can come back and take the test some other time.

VII. AT THE TEST

The day of the test is here and you have the test booklet in your hand. The temptation to get going is very strong. Caution! There is more to success than knowing the right answers. You must know how to identify your papers and understand variations in the type of short-answer question used in this particular examination. Follow these suggestions for maximum results from your efforts:

1) Cooperate with the monitor

The test administrator has a duty to create a situation in which you can be as much at ease as possible. He will give instructions, tell you when to begin, check to see that you are marking your answer sheet correctly, and so on. He is not there to guard you, although he will see that your competitors do not take unfair advantage. He wants to help you do your best.

2) Listen to all instructions

Don't jump the gun! Wait until you understand all directions. In most civil service tests you get more time than you need to answer the questions. So don't be in a hurry. Read each word of instructions until you clearly understand the meaning. Study the examples, listen to all announcements and follow directions. Ask questions if you do not understand what to do.

3) Identify your papers

Civil service exams are usually identified by number only. You will be assigned a number; you must not put your name on your test papers. Be sure to copy your number correctly. Since more than one exam may be given, copy your exact examination title.

4) Plan your time

Unless you are told that a test is a "speed" or "rate of work" test, speed itself is usually not important. Time enough to answer all the questions will be provided, but this does not mean that you have all day. An overall time limit has been set. Divide the total time (in minutes) by the number of questions to determine the approximate time you have for each question.

5) Do not linger over difficult questions

If you come across a difficult question, mark it with a paper clip (useful to have along) and come back to it when you have been through the booklet. One caution if you do this – be sure to skip a number on your answer sheet as well. Check often to be sure that you have not lost your place and that you are marking in the row numbered the same as the question you are answering.

6) Read the questions

Be sure you know what the question asks! Many capable people are unsuccessful because they failed to *read* the questions correctly.

7) Answer all questions

Unless you have been instructed that a penalty will be deducted for incorrect answers, it is better to guess than to omit a question.

8) Speed tests

It is often better NOT to guess on speed tests. It has been found that on timed tests people are tempted to spend the last few seconds before time is called in marking answers at random – without even reading them – in the hope of picking up a few extra points. To discourage this practice, the instructions may warn you that your score will be "corrected" for guessing. That is, a penalty will be applied. The incorrect answers will be deducted from the correct ones, or some other penalty formula will be used.

9) Review your answers

If you finish before time is called, go back to the questions you guessed or omitted to give them further thought. Review other answers if you have time.

10) Return your test materials

If you are ready to leave before others have finished or time is called, take ALL your materials to the monitor and leave quietly. Never take any test material with you. The monitor can discover whose papers are not complete, and taking a test booklet may be grounds for disqualification.

VIII. EXAMINATION TECHNIQUES

1) Read the general instructions carefully. These are usually printed on the first page of the exam booklet. As a rule, these instructions refer to the timing of the examination; the fact that you should not start work until the signal and must stop work at a signal, etc. If there are any *special* instructions, such as a choice of questions to be answered, make sure that you note this instruction carefully.

2) When you are ready to start work on the examination, that is as soon as the signal has been given, read the instructions to each question booklet, underline any key words or phrases, such as *least, best, outline, describe* and the like. In this way you will tend to answer as requested rather than discover on reviewing your paper that you *listed without describing*, that you selected the *worst* choice rather than the *best* choice, etc.

3) If the examination is of the objective or multiple-choice type – that is, each question will also give a series of possible answers: A, B, C or D, and you are called upon to select the best answer and write the letter next to that answer on your answer paper – it is advisable to start answering each question in turn. There may be anywhere from 50 to 100 such questions in the three or four hours allotted and you can see how much time would be taken if you read through all the questions before beginning to answer any. Furthermore, if you come across a question or group of questions which you know would be difficult to answer, it would undoubtedly affect your handling of all the other questions.

4) If the examination is of the essay type and contains but a few questions, it is a moot point as to whether you should read all the questions before starting to answer any one. Of course, if you are given a choice – say five out of seven and the like – then it is essential to read all the questions so you can eliminate the two that are most difficult. If, however, you are asked to answer all the questions, there may be danger in trying to answer the easiest one first because you may find that you will spend too much time on it. The best technique is to answer the first question, then proceed to the second, etc.

5) Time your answers. Before the exam begins, write down the time it started, then add the time allowed for the examination and write down the time it must be completed, then divide the time available somewhat as follows:
    - If 3-1/2 hours are allowed, that would be 210 minutes. If you have 80 objective-type questions, that would be an average of 2-1/2 minutes per question. Allow yourself no more than 2 minutes per question, or a total of 160 minutes, which will permit about 50 minutes to review.
    - If for the time allotment of 210 minutes there are 7 essay questions to answer, that would average about 30 minutes a question. Give yourself only 25 minutes per question so that you have about 35 minutes to review.

6) The most important instruction is to *read each question* and make sure you know what is wanted. The second most important instruction is to *time yourself properly* so that you answer every question. The third most important instruction is to *answer every question*. Guess if you have to but include something for each question. Remember that you will receive no credit for a blank and will probably receive some credit if you write something in answer to an essay question. If you guess a letter – say "B" for a multiple-choice question – you may have guessed right. If you leave a blank as an answer to a multiple-choice question, the examiners may respect your feelings but it will not add a point to your score. Some exams may penalize you for wrong answers, so in such cases *only*, you may not want to guess unless you have some basis for your answer.

7) Suggestions
    a. Objective-type questions
        1. Examine the question booklet for proper sequence of pages and questions
        2. Read all instructions carefully
        3. Skip any question which seems too difficult; return to it after all other questions have been answered
        4. Apportion your time properly; do not spend too much time on any single question or group of questions

5. Note and underline key words – *all, most, fewest, least, best, worst, same, opposite,* etc.
6. Pay particular attention to negatives
7. Note unusual option, e.g., unduly long, short, complex, different or similar in content to the body of the question
8. Observe the use of "hedging" words – *probably, may, most likely,* etc.
9. Make sure that your answer is put next to the same number as the question
10. Do not second-guess unless you have good reason to believe the second answer is definitely more correct
11. Cross out original answer if you decide another answer is more accurate; do not erase until you are ready to hand your paper in
12. Answer all questions; guess unless instructed otherwise
13. Leave time for review

b. Essay questions
1. Read each question carefully
2. Determine exactly what is wanted. Underline key words or phrases.
3. Decide on outline or paragraph answer
4. Include many different points and elements unless asked to develop any one or two points or elements
5. Show impartiality by giving pros and cons unless directed to select one side only
6. Make and write down any assumptions you find necessary to answer the questions
7. Watch your English, grammar, punctuation and choice of words
8. Time your answers; don't crowd material

8) Answering the essay question

Most essay questions can be answered by framing the specific response around several key words or ideas. Here are a few such key words or ideas:

M's: manpower, materials, methods, money, management
P's: purpose, program, policy, plan, procedure, practice, problems, pitfalls, personnel, public relations

    a. Six basic steps in handling problems:
        1. Preliminary plan and background development
        2. Collect information, data and facts
        3. Analyze and interpret information, data and facts
        4. Analyze and develop solutions as well as make recommendations
        5. Prepare report and sell recommendations
        6. Install recommendations and follow up effectiveness

    b. Pitfalls to avoid
        1. *Taking things for granted* – A statement of the situation does not necessarily imply that each of the elements is necessarily true; for example, a complaint may be invalid and biased so that all that can be taken for granted is that a complaint has been registered

2. *Considering only one side of a situation* – Wherever possible, indicate several alternatives and then point out the reasons you selected the best one
3. *Failing to indicate follow up* – Whenever your answer indicates action on your part, make certain that you will take proper follow-up action to see how successful your recommendations, procedures or actions turn out to be
4. *Taking too long in answering any single question* – Remember to time your answers properly

IX. AFTER THE TEST

Scoring procedures differ in detail among civil service jurisdictions although the general principles are the same. Whether the papers are hand-scored or graded by machine we have described, they are nearly always graded by number. That is, the person who marks the paper knows only the number – never the name – of the applicant. Not until all the papers have been graded will they be matched with names. If other tests, such as training and experience or oral interview ratings have been given, scores will be combined. Different parts of the examination usually have different weights. For example, the written test might count 60 percent of the final grade, and a rating of training and experience 40 percent. In many jurisdictions, veterans will have a certain number of points added to their grades.

After the final grade has been determined, the names are placed in grade order and an eligible list is established. There are various methods for resolving ties between those who get the same final grade – probably the most common is to place first the name of the person whose application was received first. Job offers are made from the eligible list in the order the names appear on it. You will be notified of your grade and your rank as soon as all these computations have been made. This will be done as rapidly as possible.

People who are found to meet the requirements in the announcement are called "eligibles." Their names are put on a list of eligible candidates. An eligible's chances of getting a job depend on how high he stands on this list and how fast agencies are filling jobs from the list.

When a job is to be filled from a list of eligibles, the agency asks for the names of people on the list of eligibles for that job. When the civil service commission receives this request, it sends to the agency the names of the three people highest on this list. Or, if the job to be filled has specialized requirements, the office sends the agency the names of the top three persons who meet these requirements from the general list.

The appointing officer makes a choice from among the three people whose names were sent to him. If the selected person accepts the appointment, the names of the others are put back on the list to be considered for future openings.

That is the rule in hiring from all kinds of eligible lists, whether they are for typist, carpenter, chemist, or something else. For every vacancy, the appointing officer has his choice of any one of the top three eligibles on the list. This explains why the person whose name is on top of the list sometimes does not get an appointment when some of the persons lower on the list do. If the appointing officer chooses the second or third eligible, the No. 1 eligible does not get a job at once, but stays on the list until he is appointed or the list is terminated.

X. HOW TO PASS THE INTERVIEW TEST

The examination for which you applied requires an oral interview test. You have already taken the written test and you are now being called for the interview test – the final part of the formal examination.

You may think that it is not possible to prepare for an interview test and that there are no procedures to follow during an interview. Our purpose is to point out some things you can do in advance that will help you and some good rules to follow and pitfalls to avoid while you are being interviewed.

What is an interview supposed to test?

The written examination is designed to test the technical knowledge and competence of the candidate; the oral is designed to evaluate intangible qualities, not readily measured otherwise, and to establish a list showing the relative fitness of each candidate – as measured against his competitors – for the position sought. Scoring is not on the basis of "right" and "wrong," but on a sliding scale of values ranging from "not passable" to "outstanding." As a matter of fact, it is possible to achieve a relatively low score without a single "incorrect" answer because of evident weakness in the qualities being measured.

Occasionally, an examination may consist entirely of an oral test – either an individual or a group oral. In such cases, information is sought concerning the technical knowledges and abilities of the candidate, since there has been no written examination for this purpose. More commonly, however, an oral test is used to supplement a written examination.

Who conducts interviews?

The composition of oral boards varies among different jurisdictions. In nearly all, a representative of the personnel department serves as chairman. One of the members of the board may be a representative of the department in which the candidate would work. In some cases, "outside experts" are used, and, frequently, a businessman or some other representative of the general public is asked to serve. Labor and management or other special groups may be represented. The aim is to secure the services of experts in the appropriate field.

However the board is composed, it is a good idea (and not at all improper or unethical) to ascertain in advance of the interview who the members are and what groups they represent. When you are introduced to them, you will have some idea of their backgrounds and interests, and at least you will not stutter and stammer over their names.

What should be done before the interview?

While knowledge about the board members is useful and takes some of the surprise element out of the interview, there is other preparation which is more substantive. It *is* possible to prepare for an oral interview – in several ways:

1) Keep a copy of your application and review it carefully before the interview

This may be the only document before the oral board, and the starting point of the interview. Know what education and experience you have listed there, and the sequence and dates of all of it. Sometimes the board will ask you to review the highlights of your experience for them; you should not have to hem and haw doing it.

2) Study the class specification and the examination announcement

Usually, the oral board has one or both of these to guide them. The qualities, characteristics or knowledges required by the position sought are stated in these documents. They offer valuable clues as to the nature of the oral interview. For example, if the job involves supervisory responsibilities, the announcement will usually indicate that knowledge of modern supervisory methods and the qualifications of the candidate as a supervisor will be tested. If so, you can expect such questions, frequently in the form of a hypothetical situation which you are expected to solve. NEVER go into an oral without knowledge of the duties and responsibilities of the job you seek.

3) Think through each qualification required

Try to visualize the kind of questions you would ask if you were a board member. How well could you answer them? Try especially to appraise your own knowledge and background in each area, *measured against the job sought*, and identify any areas in which you are weak. Be critical and realistic – do not flatter yourself.

4) Do some general reading in areas in which you feel you may be weak

For example, if the job involves supervision and your past experience has NOT, some general reading in supervisory methods and practices, particularly in the field of human relations, might be useful. Do NOT study agency procedures or detailed manuals. The oral board will be testing your understanding and capacity, not your memory.

5) Get a good night's sleep and watch your general health and mental attitude

You will want a clear head at the interview. Take care of a cold or any other minor ailment, and of course, no hangovers.

What should be done on the day of the interview?

Now comes the day of the interview itself. Give yourself plenty of time to get there. Plan to arrive somewhat ahead of the scheduled time, particularly if your appointment is in the fore part of the day. If a previous candidate fails to appear, the board might be ready for you a bit early. By early afternoon an oral board is almost invariably behind schedule if there are many candidates, and you may have to wait. Take along a book or magazine to read, or your application to review, but leave any extraneous material in the waiting room when you go in for your interview. In any event, relax and compose yourself.

The matter of dress is important. The board is forming impressions about you – from your experience, your manners, your attitude, and your appearance. Give your personal appearance careful attention. Dress your best, but not your flashiest. Choose conservative, appropriate clothing, and be sure it is immaculate. This is a business interview, and your appearance should indicate that you regard it as such. Besides, being well groomed and properly dressed will help boost your confidence.

Sooner or later, someone will call your name and escort you into the interview room. *This is it.* From here on you are on your own. It is too late for any more preparation. But remember, you asked for this opportunity to prove your fitness, and you are here because your request was granted.

What happens when you go in?

The usual sequence of events will be as follows: The clerk (who is often the board stenographer) will introduce you to the chairman of the oral board, who will introduce you to the other members of the board. Acknowledge the introductions before you sit down. Do not be surprised if you find a microphone facing you or a stenotypist sitting by. Oral interviews are usually recorded in the event of an appeal or other review.

Usually the chairman of the board will open the interview by reviewing the highlights of your education and work experience from your application – primarily for the benefit of the other members of the board, as well as to get the material into the record. Do not interrupt or comment unless there is an error or significant misinterpretation; if that is the case, do not hesitate. But do not quibble about insignificant matters. Also, he will usually ask you some question about your education, experience or your present job – partly to get you to start talking and to establish the interviewing "rapport." He may start the actual questioning, or turn it over to one of the other members. Frequently, each member undertakes the questioning on a particular area, one in which he is perhaps most competent, so you can expect each member to participate in the examination. Because time is limited, you may also expect some rather abrupt switches in the direction the questioning takes, so do not be upset by it. Normally, a board member will not pursue a single line of questioning unless he discovers a particular strength or weakness.

After each member has participated, the chairman will usually ask whether any member has any further questions, then will ask you if you have anything you wish to add. Unless you are expecting this question, it may floor you. Worse, it may start you off on an extended, extemporaneous speech. The board is not usually seeking more information. The question is principally to offer you a last opportunity to present further qualifications or to indicate that you have nothing to add. So, if you feel that a significant qualification or characteristic has been overlooked, it is proper to point it out in a sentence or so. Do not compliment the board on the thoroughness of their examination – they have been sketchy, and you know it. If you wish, merely say, "No thank you, I have nothing further to add." This is a point where you can "talk yourself out" of a good impression or fail to present an important bit of information. Remember, *you close the interview yourself*.

The chairman will then say, "That is all, Mr. _____, thank you." Do not be startled; the interview is over, and quicker than you think. Thank him, gather your belongings and take your leave. Save your sigh of relief for the other side of the door.

How to put your best foot forward
Throughout this entire process, you may feel that the board individually and collectively is trying to pierce your defenses, seek out your hidden weaknesses and embarrass and confuse you. Actually, this is not true. They are obliged to make an appraisal of your qualifications for the job you are seeking, and they want to see you in your best light. Remember, they must interview all candidates and a non-cooperative candidate may become a failure in spite of their best efforts to bring out his qualifications. Here are 15 suggestions that will help you:

1) Be natural – Keep your attitude confident, not cocky
If you are not confident that you can do the job, do not expect the board to be. Do not apologize for your weaknesses, try to bring out your strong points. The board is interested in a positive, not negative, presentation. Cockiness will antagonize any board member and make him wonder if you are covering up a weakness by a false show of strength.

2) Get comfortable, but don't lounge or sprawl
Sit erectly but not stiffly. A careless posture may lead the board to conclude that you are careless in other things, or at least that you are not impressed by the importance of the occasion. Either conclusion is natural, even if incorrect. Do not fuss with your clothing, a pencil or an ashtray. Your hands may occasionally be useful to emphasize a point; do not let them become a point of distraction.

3) Do not wisecrack or make small talk
This is a serious situation, and your attitude should show that you consider it as such. Further, the time of the board is limited – they do not want to waste it, and neither should you.

4) Do not exaggerate your experience or abilities

In the first place, from information in the application or other interviews and sources, the board may know more about you than you think. Secondly, you probably will not get away with it. An experienced board is rather adept at spotting such a situation, so do not take the chance.

5) If you know a board member, do not make a point of it, yet do not hide it

Certainly you are not fooling him, and probably not the other members of the board. Do not try to take advantage of your acquaintanceship – it will probably do you little good.

6) Do not dominate the interview

Let the board do that. They will give you the clues – do not assume that you have to do all the talking. Realize that the board has a number of questions to ask you, and do not try to take up all the interview time by showing off your extensive knowledge of the answer to the first one.

7) Be attentive

You only have 20 minutes or so, and you should keep your attention at its sharpest throughout. When a member is addressing a problem or question to you, give him your undivided attention. Address your reply principally to him, but do not exclude the other board members.

8) Do not interrupt

A board member may be stating a problem for you to analyze. He will ask you a question when the time comes. Let him state the problem, and wait for the question.

9) Make sure you understand the question

Do not try to answer until you are sure what the question is. If it is not clear, restate it in your own words or ask the board member to clarify it for you. However, do not haggle about minor elements.

10) Reply promptly but not hastily

A common entry on oral board rating sheets is "candidate responded readily," or "candidate hesitated in replies." Respond as promptly and quickly as you can, but do not jump to a hasty, ill-considered answer.

11) Do not be peremptory in your answers

A brief answer is proper – but do not fire your answer back. That is a losing game from your point of view. The board member can probably ask questions much faster than you can answer them.

12) Do not try to create the answer you think the board member wants

He is interested in what kind of mind you have and how it works – not in playing games. Furthermore, he can usually spot this practice and will actually grade you down on it.

13) Do not switch sides in your reply merely to agree with a board member

Frequently, a member will take a contrary position merely to draw you out and to see if you are willing and able to defend your point of view. Do not start a debate, yet do not surrender a good position. If a position is worth taking, it is worth defending.

14) Do not be afraid to admit an error in judgment if you are shown to be wrong

The board knows that you are forced to reply without any opportunity for careful consideration. Your answer may be demonstrably wrong. If so, admit it and get on with the interview.

15) Do not dwell at length on your present job

The opening question may relate to your present assignment. Answer the question but do not go into an extended discussion. You are being examined for a *new* job, not your present one. As a matter of fact, try to phrase ALL your answers in terms of the job for which you are being examined.

Basis of Rating

Probably you will forget most of these "do's" and "don'ts" when you walk into the oral interview room. Even remembering them all will not ensure you a passing grade. Perhaps you did not have the qualifications in the first place. But remembering them will help you to put your best foot forward, without treading on the toes of the board members.

Rumor and popular opinion to the contrary notwithstanding, an oral board wants you to make the best appearance possible. They know you are under pressure – but they also want to see how you respond to it as a guide to what your reaction would be under the pressures of the job you seek. They will be influenced by the degree of poise you display, the personal traits you show and the manner in which you respond.

ABOUT THIS BOOK

This book contains tests divided into Examination Sections. Go through each test, answering every question in the margin. We have also attached a sample answer sheet at the back of the book that can be removed and used. At the end of each test look at the answer key and check your answers. On the ones you got wrong, look at the right answer choice and learn. Do not fill in the answers first. Do not memorize the questions and answers, but understand the answer and principles involved. On your test, the questions will likely be different from the samples. Questions are changed and new ones added. If you understand these past questions you should have success with any changes that arise. Tests may consist of several types of questions. We have additional books on each subject should more study be advisable or necessary for you. Finally, the more you study, the better prepared you will be. This book is intended to be the last thing you study before you walk into the examination room. Prior study of relevant texts is also recommended. NLC publishes some of these in our Fundamental Series. Knowledge and good sense are important factors in passing your exam. Good luck also helps. So now study this Passbook, absorb the material contained within and take that knowledge into the examination. Then do your best to pass that exam.

EXAMINATION SECTION

EXAMINATION SECTION
TEST 1

DIRECTIONS: Each question or incomplete statement is followed by several suggested answers or completions. Select the one that BEST answers the question or completes the statement. *PRINT THE LETTER OF THE CORRECT ANSWER IN THE SPACE AT THE RIGHT.*

1. Chlorophyll may be extracted from leaves by boiling the leaves in 1.____
   A. alcohol
   B. benzene
   C. dilute acetic acid
   D. water

2. To dehydrate a specimen, it is BEST to use 2.____
   A. absolute alcohol
   B. gum Arabic
   C. turpentine
   D. xylol

3. To destroy sucking insects on laboratory plants, it is BEST to use 3.____
   A. flit
   B. rotenone
   C. soap solution
   D. 2-4D

4. The thoracic duct is part of the 4.____
   A. heart
   B. lymphatic system
   C. respiratory system
   D. umbilical cord

5. Of the following, the substance which should NOT be used to slow down the activity of paramecia on a microscope slide is 5.____
   A. absorbent cotton
   B. ether
   C. lens paper
   D. methyl cellulose

6. The oil used with an oil-immersion microscope is 6.____
   A. cedarwood
   B. clove
   C. light machine
   D. olive

7. Frogs may be prepared for dissection by 7.____
   A. boiling them gently
   B. etherizing them
   C. freezing them
   D. soaking in formaldehyde

8. Nitrogen-fixing bacteria may be found on the roots of 8.____
   A. clover   B. geranium   C. sunflower   D. timothy

9. Of the following, the BEST substance to use to reveal the cell membrane in onion cells is 9.____
   A. concentrated saline
   B. ink
   C. iodine stain
   D. Wright's stain

10. Chloroplasts may be seen by setting up a microscope demonstration of
    A. elodea cells
    B. leaf epidermis cells
    C. onion skin cells
    D. paramecia

11. Scarification is used in
    A. planting seeds
    B. pollinating flowers
    C. preparing seeds for planting
    D. preparing the seed bed

12. To demonstrate the movement of cytoplasmic structures, one might BEST use cells of
    A. elodea   B. geranium   C. potato   D. the cheek

13. Of the following, the plant which would be a POOR choice for a freshwater aquarium is
    A. cabomba   B. elodea   C. fucus   D. vallismeria

14. To pith a frog,
    A. cut off its head
    B. insert a needle in its brain
    C. rub mild acid on its leg
    D. stimulate with an electric current

15. Crowded cultures in which the food supply has diminished usually result in cannibalism in
    A. amoeba
    B. blepharisma
    C. paramecium
    D. vorticella

16. Zygospores can be demonstrated in
    A. amphioxus
    B. bacillus subtilis
    C. paramecium
    D. spirogyra

17. Pure agar contains sufficient nutrient material to culture
    A. few, if any, organisms
    B. most algae
    C. most bacteria
    D. most molds

18. An example of a motile unicellular plant is a
    A. coccus   B. desmid   C. diatom   D. yeast

19. A good loop for bacteriological work may be made of
    A. copper   B. catgut   C. invar   D. nichrome

20. Petri dishes may BEST be sterilized before use in
    A. the Arnold sterilizer
    B. the autoclave
    C. the hot air oven
    D. lysol

21. In order to demonstrate protoplasmic movement, it is good practice, before placing a slide of elodea under the microscope, to
    A. add a few drops of a paramecium culture
    B. expose the plant to an electric light
    C. keep the plant at a low temperature
    D. keep the plant in the dark

22. Under similar conditions, the slowest moving protozoan in the following group would be
    A. ameba   B. blepharisma   C. colpoda   D. paramecium

22.____

23. Radiocarbon 14 dating provides a timetable that covers the last _____ years.
    A. few thousand   B. few hundred thousand
    C. million   D. ten million

23.____

24. Bacteria generally reproduce by
    A. conjugation   B. fertilization
    C. fission   D. vegetative propagation

24.____

25. The gland whose removal prevents metamorphosis in the frog is the
    A. adrenal   B. pancreas   C. pineal   D. thyroid

25.____

KEY (CORRECT ANSWERS)

1.	A	11.	C
2.	A	12.	A
3.	B	13.	C
4.	B	14.	B
5.	B	15.	B
6.	A	16.	D
7.	B	17.	A
8.	A	18.	C
9.	A	19.	D
10.	A	20.	C

21. B
22. A
23. A
24. C
25. D

TEST 2

DIRECTIONS: Each question or incomplete statement is followed by several suggested answers or completions. Select the one that BEST answers the question or completes the statement. *PRINT THE LETTER OF THE CORRECT ANSWER IN THE SPACE AT THE RIGHT.*

1. A shrub that flowers normally in the late fall is the   1.____
    A. blueberry   B. high bush cranberry
    C. mock orange   D. witch hazel

2. To secure epithelial cells from the inside of the cheek, use   2.____
    A. a sterilized needle   B. a sterilized coverslip
    C. the blunt edge of a sterile scalpel   D. the blunt edge of a toothpick

3. In mounting butterflies, the pin is usually inserted   3.____
    A. between the head and thorax
    B. near the bottom end of the abdomen
    C. through the center of the thorax
    D. through the right wing

4. To separate female drosophila for crossing, choose flies which have a _____ abdomen.   4.____
    A. black-tipped   B. broad-spotted
    C. broad-striped   D. small spotted

5. A good place to get a supply of paramecia for culturing in the laboratory is in   5.____
    A. a running stream   B. a stagnant pond
    C. brackish water   D. the Hudson River

6. To obtain conjugation in the common bread mold (Rhizopus), it is necessary to have   6.____
    A. asexual spores from different hyphae
    B. plus and minus strains
    C. two groups of sporangia
    D. two mycelia

7. An adhesive which will affix paraffin sections or microorganisms to slides is commonly made from   7.____
    A. egg albumin   B. rubber cement
    C. flour and water   D. starch paste

8. Hay is usually used in a medium for culturing   8.____
    A. fruit flies   B. protozoa   C. planaria   D. molds

9. Wrinkled paraffin sections of tissues may be flattened by   9.____
    A. adding alcohol   B. adding xylol
    C. placing them on a warming table   D. using a detergent

10. To show the effect of an enzyme, one could use milk and	10.____
    A. HCl	B. pepsin	C. rennin	D. secretin

11. Cuttings which develop roots MOST quickly are those of	11.____
    A. elm	B. maple	C. oak	D. willow

12. In testing for glucose, which one of the following is useful?	12.____
    A. Benedict's solution	B. Lugol's solution
    C. Nitric acid	D. Sucrose

13. The number of smooth peas to use with one wrinkled pea in a Riker mount	13.____
    which is to illustrate the mating of hybrids (smooth dominant, wrinkled
    recessive) is
    A. one	B. two	C. three	D. four

14. The species which has leaves lacking tooth-like points is the	14.____
    A. red oak	B. white oak
    C. American elm	D. sugar maple

15. From an infusion of unwashed grapes in water, one may usually get a good	15.____
    culture of
    A. euglena	B. mixed ciliates
    C. paramecia	D. yeast

16. To get a number of small plants from a leaf, one would use the leaf of	16.____
    A. Bryophyllum	B. butter-and-eggs (Linaria)
    C. geranium	D. ragweed

17. Of the following, the leaves which BEST show variation in form are	17.____
    A. elm	B. flowering dogwood
    C. Norway maple	D. sassafras

18. A Coplin jar is generally used for	18.____
    A. copper-plating	B. culturing protozoa
    C. staining slides	D. storing preserved animals

19. A characteristic by which the male dog can be distinguished from the female is	19.____
    A. red tongue	B. spot on the head
    C. very thick thumbs	D. web-feet

20. The organ of Corti is found in the	20.____
    A. adrenal gland	B. ear	C. eye	D. liver

21. A chemical used to dehydrate and clear specimens is	21.____
    A. alcohol	B. methyl green	C. nigrosine	D. xylol

22. A camera lucida is a device that is helpful in
    A. clearing objects for microscopic study
    B. making drawings of microscopic objects
    C. making lantern slide transparencies
    D. taking photomicrographs

23. The motion of small cocci in a sealed hanging drop is generally due to
    A. amoeboid motion   B. action of flagellae
    C. Brownian movement   D. ciliary movement

24. For demonstrating centrosomes and spindles, a laboratory assistant should make available slides of
    A. early cleavage stages of whitefish eggs
    B. human cheek epithelial cells
    C. mitosis in onion root tips
    D. pollen mother cells in sections of anthers

25. A substance that is NOT used in the modern treatment of severe burns is
    A. blood   B. cortisone   C. penicillin   D. tannic acid

KEY (CORRECT ANSWERS)

1.	D	11.	D
2.	D	12.	A
3.	C	13.	C
4.	C	14.	B
5.	B	15.	D
6.	B	16.	A
7.	A	17.	D
8.	B	18.	C
9.	C	19.	C
10.	C	20.	B

21. D
22. B
23. C
24. A
25. D

TEST 3

DIRECTIONS: Each question or incomplete statement is followed by several suggested answers or completions. Select the one that BEST answers the question or completes the statement. *PRINT THE LETTER OF THE CORRECT ANSWER IN THE SPACE AT THE RIGHT.*

1. The theory of Use and Disuse was proposed by 1.____
   A. De Vries B. La Farge C. Lamarck D. Thales

2. ACTH is a(n) 2.____
   A. autacoid B. enzyme C. hormone D. vitamin

3. A recently discovered hoax was _____ man. 3.____
   A. Java B. Neanderthal C. Piltdown D. Texepan

4. To discover whether a trait in an organism is dominant, the organism should be crossed with a 4.____
   A. hybrid dominant
   B. hybrid recessive
   C. pure dominant
   D. pure recessive

5. Chromosomes do not occur in pairs in 5.____
   A. body cells
   B. fertilized eggs
   C. gametes
   D. zygotes

6. Chemotherapy (the use of chemicals in the treatment of disease) had its inception with 6.____
   A. Ehrlich
   B. Madame Curie
   C. Paracelsus
   D. Park

7. The gland which produces insulin is to be found in the 7.____
   A. liver B. pancreas C. pituitary D. thymus

8. Deoxygenated blood enters the heart at the 8.____
   A. left auricle
   B. left ventricle
   C. right auricle
   D. right ventricle

9. Of the following, the item which is NOT properly grouped with the remaining three is 9.____
   A. chromosome
   B. centrosome
   C. spindle fiber
   D. muscle fiber

10. In tracer studies, radioiodine would be concentrated in the 10.____
    A. adrenals B. liver C. pituitary D. thyroid

11. The sex chromosome combination of a human male is 11.____
    A. XO B. XX C. XY D. YY

12. Most plant and animal cells are similar in that they both have
    A. cytoplasm and cellulose
    B. cytoplasm and contractile vacuole
    C. cytoplasm and nucleus
    D. membrane and cell wall

13. Saponification in the small intestine is the direct result of the action of
    A. bile   B. lacteals   C. secretin   D. villein

14. Of the following "men," the one with the LARGEST brain case was
    A. Cro-Magnon   B. Heidelberg   C. Java   D. Peking

15. Of the following, the one non-antibiotic is
    A. gramicidin   B. streptomycin   C. sympathin   D. terramycin

16. Amongst the following, the SMALLEST in size is the
    A. bacillus   B. coccus   C. rickettsia   D. virus

17. Of the following, the item which is not properly grouped with the remaining three is
    A. thrombin   B. fibrin   C. vitamin K   D. vitamin B_2

18. Tx × Tt in which T is the dominant will result in a
    A. 1:1 ratio
    B. 3:1 ratio
    C. 9:3:3:1 ratio
    D. 100% of the dominant

19. In general, the size of an animal's egg depends on the
    A. amount of cytoplasm
    B. amount of yolk
    C. rate of development
    D. size of nucleus

20. A "blue baby" may result from the mating of an Rh _____ male and Rh _____ female.
    A. positive; positive
    B. negative; positive
    C. positive; negative
    D. negative; negative

21. Since barbiturates cause a paralysis of skeletal muscle, they must block impulses moving from
    A. the autonomic nervous system to muscles
    B. the central nervous system to muscles
    C. muscles to the autonomic nervous system
    D. muscles to the central nervous system

22. A drop of human blood which does not clump in either A or anti B serums is
    A. A   B. B   C. AB   D. O

23. If the chromosome number of a frog is 26, the number of chromosomes contained in its sperm is
    A. 13   B. 26   C. 39   D. 52

24. The MOST effective farming method for returning minerals to the soil is 24.____
    A. contour plowing B. crop rotation
    C. strip farming D. terracing

25. The essential parts of a flower are 25.____
    A. ovary and petals B. ovary and sepals
    C. pistils and stamens D. stamens and stigmas

KEY (CORRECT ANSWERS)

1.	C	11.	C
2.	C	12.	C
3.	C	13.	A
4.	D	14.	A
5.	C	15.	C
6.	A	16.	D
7.	B	17.	D
8.	C	18.	B
9.	D	19.	B
10.	D	20.	C

21. B
22. D
23. A
24. B
25. C

TEST 4

DIRECTIONS: Each question or incomplete statement is followed by several suggested answers or completions. Select the one that BEST answers the question or completes the statement. *PRINT THE LETTER OF THE CORRECT ANSWER IN THE SPACE AT THE RIGHT.*

1. The hormone cortisone is produced by the
   A. anterior pituitary
   B. cortex of the adrenals
   C. medulla of the adrenals
   D. posterior pituitary

   1.____

2. From among the following, the CLOSEST definition of an instinct is a
   A. conditioned reflex
   B. habit]
   C. series of reflexes
   D. none of the above

   2.____

3. The vitamin which functions in the elaboration of prothrombin in the liver is
   A. A   B. B_{12} C. C   D. K

   3.____

4. Gamma globulins used in the protection against measles and polio contain
   A. antibodies
   B. dead viruses
   C. toxoids
   D. weakened viruses

   4.____

5. The cattalo is superior in size and strength to either its cow or bison parent. This superiority is a result of
   A. hybridization   B. inbreeding   C. mutation   D. selection

   5.____

6. The MOST highly oxygenated blood in the body is found in the
   A. aorta
   B. carotid artery
   C. pulmonary artery
   D. pulmonary vein

   6.____

7. An example of symbiotic relationship is the
   A. dodder   B. earthworm   C. lichen   D. tapeworm

   7.____

8. Foods are irradiated in order to increase their content of vitamin
   A. A   B. B   C. C   D. D

   8.____

9. Giantism is the result of
   A. oversecretion of adrenal glands
   B. oversecretion of pituitary gland
   C. undersecretion of thyroid gland
   D. undersecretion of parathyroid glands

   9.____

10. In order to reduce the incidence of dental caries, the ingredient added to drinking water is
    A. bromides   B. chlorides   C. fluorides   D. iodides

    10.____

11. A "disease" which may be prevented by wearing shoes is caused by
    A. hookworm
    B. mealy worm
    C. tapeworm
    D. trichina worm

    11.____

12. The end products of protein digestion are
    A. amino acids B. glucose
    C. glycerol D. none of the above

13. Blinking in response to bright light is an example of
    A. a habit B. an instinct
    C. phototropism D. a reflex

14. Of the following, the man who made the MOST recent discoveries in genetics is
    A. Mendel B. Metchnikoff C. Morgan D. Muller

15. The chromosome number of the fruitfly is normally 8. It might be 16 if it were not kept down by the process of
    A. conjugation B. maturation
    C. mitosis D. parthenogenesis

16. A structure of the paramecium which enables it to get rid of wastes is the
    A. cell membrane B. chondriosome
    C. gullet D. trichocyst

17. Muller is known for his work in producing mutations MAINLY in
    A. corn B. fruitflies
    C. Neurospora D. planaria

18. A new TB drug is
    A. isobutanol B. isoniazid
    C. isonicotinic acid D. niacin

19. In the United States, the GREATEST percentage of the population is of blood type
    A. A B. B C. AB D. Rh positive

20. Pancreatic juice acts in the presence of
    A. HCl B. H_2CO_3 C. Na_2CO_3 D. NaCl

21. In the process of fermentation of yeast, the products formed are
    A. carbon dioxide and alcohol B. carbon dioxide and water
    C. oxygen and alcohol D. oxygen and glucose

22. The STRONGEST ciliary movement on a paramecium occurs around the
    A. anal spot B. contractile vacuole
    C. mouth D. food vacuole

23. Typhus is caused by
    A. bacteria B. protozoa C. rickettsiae D. viruses

24. After birth, the body is MOST limited in forming new _____ cells.
    A. blood B. bone C. nerve D. skin

25. A large mammal now extinct is the 25.____
    A. Archeopteryx   B. Brontosaurus
    C. mammoth   D. platypus

KEY (CORRECT ANSWERS)

1.	B		11.	A
2.	C		12.	A
3.	D		13.	D
4.	A		14.	D
5.	A		15.	B
6.	D		16.	A
7.	C		17.	B
8.	D		18.	B
9.	B		19.	D
10.	C		20.	C

21. A
22. C
23. C
24. C
25. C

TEST 5

DIRECTIONS: Each question or incomplete statement is followed by several suggested answers or completions. Select the one that BEST answers the question or completes the statement. *PRINT THE LETTER OF THE CORRECT ANSWER IN THE SPACE AT THE RIGHT.*

1. Coenzyme I is useful in
   A. digestion B. excretion C. respiration D. transpiration

2. Mapping of chromosomes is based on the percentage of
   A. crossover B. epistasis C. mutation D. polyploidy

3. The Gingko is a
   A. coniferous plant B. fern
   C. flowering plant D. none of the above

4. Fractionation of the blood was developed by
   A. Cohn B. Harvey
   C. Landsteiner D. Levine

5. To delay the blooming of chrysanthemums, the method MOST likely to be effective is to
   A. add auxins
   B. increase the number of hours of light
   C. remove auxins
   D. shorten the number of hours of light

6. The element which chlorophyll includes in its molecule is
   A. copper b. iron C. magnesium D. manganese

7. The fovea of the eye
   A. contains rods and cones B. is the blind spot in night vision
   C. is the blind spot in daylight vision D. is the blind spot in night vision

8. Studies of muscle respiration show the reaction involved in contraction is similar to
   A. aerobic respiration by yeasts B. burning of a candle
   C. fermentation by yeasts D. none of the above

9. Of the following, the part of the cell which contains the LARGEST amount of desoxyribonucleic acid is
   A. centrosome B. cytoplasm C. nucleus D. mitochondria

10. Tracer studies indicate the life of an erythrocyte is approximately _____ days.
    A. 30 B. 60 C. 90 D. 120

11. In muscle metabolism, oxygen is utilized during
    A. contraction
    B. the latent period
    C. relaxation
    D. rest

12. An example of a substance which acts as an anti-vitamin is
    A. benzoic acid
    B. choline
    C. paraminobenzoic acid
    D. sulfanilamide

13. Auremycin was developed by
    A. Dubos   B. Duggar   C. Florey   D. Waksman

14. Squids and octopuses are classified as
    A. arthropods
    B. coelenterates
    C. crustaceae
    D. mollusks

15. In cell metabolism, thiamin is active as part of a(n)
    A. enzyme   B. gene   C. hormone   D. vitamin

16. Of the following, the one that has the LARGEST number of types of cells is
    A. blood
    B. liver
    C. mouth lining
    D. muscle

17. One function of the spleen is the storage of
    A. acetylcholine
    B. dead epithelial cells
    C. folic acid
    D. red blood cells

18. A stimulant for a more rapid rate of breathing is
    A. decrease in glucose
    B. decrease in oxygen
    C. increase in carbon dioxide
    D. increase in glucose

19. Thromboplastin is a substance related to
    A. blood clotting
    B. food making
    C. green plastids
    D. sympathin E

20. Two of the MOST potent toxins are those of botulism and
    A. cholera   B. diphtheria   C. tetanus   D. typhoid

21. Ringing a tree removes the bark and the
    A. palisades layers
    B. phloem
    C. pith
    D. xylem

22. Of the following, penicillin is MOST effective against
    A. gram positive bacteria
    B. gram negative bacteria
    C. protozoa
    D. viruses

23. Desoxycorticosterone is produced in the
    A. anterior pituitary
    B. cortex of the adrenal gland
    C. cortex of the brain
    D. medulla

24. Elodea, the aquarium plant, is classified among 24.____
    A. algae   B. fungi   C. mosses   D. seed plants

25. Progesterone is produced by the 25.____
    A. anterior pituitary   B. corpus luteum
    C. posterior pituitary   D. testis

KEY (CORRECT ANSWERS)

1. C
2. A
3. A
4. A
5. B

6. C
7. D
8. C
9. C
10. D

11. C
12. D
13. B
14. D
15. A

16. B
17. D
18. C
19. A
20. C

21. B
22. A
23. B
24. D
25. B

EXAMINATION SECTION

TEST 1

DIRECTIONS: Each question or incomplete statement is followed by several suggested answers or completions. Select the one that BEST answers the question or completes the statement. *PRINT THE LETTER OF THE CORRECT ANSWER IN THE SPACE AT THE RIGHT.*

1. To avoid destructive heating effects in the use of a microprojector, one should employ
    A. a closed diaphragm
    B. copper sulfate solution
    C. light of low intensity
    D. a series of prisms

    1._____

2. The motion of small cocci in a sealed hanging drop is due generally to
    A. action of flagellae
    B. ciliary movement
    C. Brownian motion
    D. amoeboid motion

    2._____

3. A characteristic by which the male frog can be distinguished from the female is its
    A. red tongue
    B. spot on the head
    C. web-feet
    D. thick thumbs

    3._____

4. A coplin jar is generally used for
    A. culturing protozoa
    B. staining slides
    C. storing preserved animals
    D. holding dissection instruments

    4._____

5. The species of tree which has leaves lacking tooth-like points is the
    A. red oak
    B. sugar maple
    C. white oak
    D. American elm

    5._____

6. Hay is frequently used in a medium for culturing
    A. fruit flies   B. protozoa   C. planaria   D. molds

    6._____

7. To affix paraffin sections or microorganisms to slides, one should use an adhesive made from
    A. starch paste
    B. rubber cement
    C. egg albumin
    D. iron glue

    7._____

8. The nutrient that is used in the body as a source of energy and as a raw material for growth and repair is
    A. carbohydrate   B. fat   C. lipoid   D. protein

    8._____

9. An organism which can be used to show trichocysts is the
    A. starfish   B. ameba   C. paramecium   D. hydra

    9._____

10. Excess carbohydrate is stored in the human body in the form of
    A. glycerin   B. glycogen   C. glucose   D. chlorophyll

    10._____

11. A bird which does not build its own nest is the
    A. hummingbird   B. pigeon   C. orchard oriole   D. cowbird

12. Zygospores can be demonstrated in
    A. polio virus   B. paramecia   C. amphioxus   D. spirogyra

13. The hormone that stimulates the liver to release sugar into the blood is
    A. adrenin   B. insulin   C. pituitrin   D. tethelin

14. To demonstrate satisfactorily the movement of cytoplasmic structures, one should use cells of
    A. geranium   B. elodea   C. potato   D. the cheek

15. Alveoli are cavities found in the
    A. lungs   B. heart   C. liver   D. kidneys

16. An example of a plant that is usually reproduced by vegetative propagation is the
    A. potato   B. bean   C. radish   D. wheat

17. Normally, chlorophyll should be extracted from leaves by boiling the leaves in
    A. Lugol's solution   B. alcohol
    C. formaldehyde   D. hydrazine

18. If cedar oil is employed with the immersion oil objective of a microscope, the objective should be cleaned with
    A. water   B. alcohol   C. xylol   D. glycerine

19. Because of the large size of its essential organs and simple structure, a flower suitable for study is the
    A. orchid   B. sweet pea   C. rose   D. gladiolus

20. Fermentation in the laboratory may be demonstrated by a mixture of yeast and
    A. molasses   B. limewater   C. alcohol   D. carbon dioxide

21. To remove balsam from a cracked microscope slide, one should soak the slide in
    A. xylol   B. alcohol   C. water   D. glycerine

22. A laboratory demonstration with the tail of a live goldfish would prove helpful in the study of
    A. respiration   B. circulation
    C. digestion   D. glandular secretion

23. In using an autoclave, one should
    A. remove the gasket before closing the cover
    B. preheat for 60 minutes at 60 pounds pressure
    C. let some steam escape before closing the valve
    D. open the valve immediately after sterilization

24. A laboratory reagent containing copper sulfate, Rochelle salts and sodium hydroxide is
    A. Schweitzer's reagent
    B. Benedict's solution
    C. Fehling's solution
    D. Nessler's reagent

25. In grafting, the cells of each stem which would be in contact with one another are the
    A. cortical   B. cambium   C. lignin   D. phloem

KEY (CORRECT ANSWERS)

1.	B	11.	D
2.	C	12.	D
3.	D	13.	A
4.	B	14.	B
5.	C	15.	A
6.	B	16.	A
7.	C	17.	B
8.	D	18.	C
9.	C	19.	D
10.	B	20.	A

21.	A
22.	B
23.	C
24.	C
25.	B

TEST 2

DIRECTIONS: Each question or incomplete statement is followed by several suggested answers or completions. Select the one that BEST answers the question or completes the statement. *PRINT THE LETTER OF THE CORRECT ANSWER IN THE SPACE AT THE RIGHT.*

1. To provide immunity against diphtheria, a healthy child is inoculated with 1.____
   A. toxoid B. toxin C. antitoxin D. germicide

2. The plant tissue which normally conducts food from leaves down to the roots is the 2.____
   A. pith B. tracheid C. phloem D. cambium

3. Chloroplasts may be observed by means of a microscope demonstration of 3.____
   A. onion skill cells B. ameba
   C. elodea cells D. leaf epidermis cells

4. The part of the brain that controls the breathing reflex is the 4.____
   A. cerebrum B. cerebellum C. meninges D. medulla

5. In the classification of living things, proceeding from the largest grouping down to the smallest, the CORRECT choice is: 5.____
   A. Phylum – class – order – genus – species
   B. Phylum – class – order – species – genus
   C. Phylum – genus – class – order – species
   D. Phylum – order – class – genus - species

6. In the normal use of the microscope, light will strike the mirror and then proceed as follows: 6.____
   A. Slide – objective – ocular – lens of eye
   B. Slide – lens of eye – objective – ocular
   C. Slide – ocular – objective – lens of eye
   D. Slide – lens of eye – ocular - objective

7. When air is inhaled, all of the following activities take place EXCEPT the 7.____
   A. diaphragm contracts B. ribs are raised
   C. chest cavity is enlarged D. lungs contract

8. Another name for grain alcohol is _____ alcohol. 8.____
   A. wood B. methyl C. ethyl D. amyl

9. Oxyhemoglobin differs from hemoglobin in that it contains _____ oxygen. 9.____
   A. less B. more
   C. same amount of D. no

10. The normal order of events in the clotting of blood is:
    A. Platelets – fibrin – fibrinogen – thrombin
    B. Platelets – thrombin – fibrinogen – fibrin
    C. Fibrinogen – fibrin – platelets – thrombin
    D. Fibrinogen – platelets – thrombin - fibrin

11. The tiny particles within the nucleus of a cell are known as
    A. centrosomes   B. hypertonic salts
    C. chromatin   D. parenchyma

12. Cancer cells that spread throughout the body are called
    A. phagocytes   B. opsonins   C. metastases   D. lymphocytes

13. Viruses have been photographed through the use of the
    A. interferometer   B. polariscope
    C. electron microscope D. spectroscope

14. The hormone which increases the rate of oxidation in the cells of the body is
    A. insulin   B. thyroxin   C. pituitrin   D. progestin

15. The carbohydrate which the body cells can oxidize MOST readily is
    A. galactose   B. fructose   C. glucose   D. sucrose

16. The thoracic duct is part of the
    A. lymphatic system   B. heart
    C. appendix   D. respiratory system

17. Maple and milkweed fruits may be used to demonstrate
    A. asexual reproduction B. regeneration
    C. appendix   D. respiratory system

18. An example of a motile unicellular plant is a
    A. coccus   B. yeast   C. desmid   D. diatom

19. The gland whose removal prevents metamorphosis in the frog is the
    A. thyroid   B. adrenal   C. pineal   D. pancreas

20. A satisfactory source for obtaining paramecia for culturing in the laboratory is
    A. a stagnant pond   B. a running stream
    C. tap water   D. an underground river

21. To demonstrate enzymatic action, one could use milk and
    A. pepsin   B. secretin   C. rennin   D. catalase

22. An infusion of unwashed grapes in water generally yields a satisfactory culture of
    A. hydra   B. euglena   C. paramecia   D. yeast

23. To illustrate regeneration, one should use the   23.____
    A. planarian   B. lobster   C. cyclops   D. paramecium

24. Parthenogenesis is the development of the embryo from a(n)   24.____
    A. fertilized egg   B. zygote
    C. zygospore   D. unfertilized egg

25. Of the following, the ion not found in Ringer's solution is the _____ ion.   25.____
    A. sodium   B. chloride   C. bicarbonate   D. potassium

KEY (CORRECT ANSWERS)

1.	A	11.	C
2.	C	12.	C
3.	C	13.	C
4.	D	14.	B
5.	A	15.	C
6.	A	16.	A
7.	D	17.	D
8.	C	18.	D
9.	B	19.	A
10.	B	20.	A

21. C
22. D
23. A
24. D
25. C

TEST 3

DIRECTIONS: Each question or incomplete statement is followed by several suggested answers or completions. Select the one that BEST answers the question or completes the statement. *PRINT THE LETTER OF THE CORRECT ANSWER IN THE SPACE AT THE RIGHT.*

1. Pollen grains may be made to germinate on a slide containing
   A. auxin
   B. hydroponic solution
   C. sugar solution
   D. thyroxin

   1.____

2. After use, the oil-immersion lens of a microscope should be cleaned gently with
   A. xylol
   B. dilute sodium hydroxide
   C. dilute sulfuric acid
   D. glycerine

   2.____

3. When cheek cells are to be removed for microscopic study in the laboratory, one should employ a(n)
   A. dissecting needle
   B. sharp scalpel
   C. toothpick
   D. microtome

   3.____

4. A slide of plant cells may be made readily by using
   A. carrot
   B. corn stalk
   C. onion
   D. potato

   4.____

5. Bread mold will grow MOST satisfactorily if the bread is
   A. kept dry
   B. kept moist
   C. sterilized
   D. kept in the sun

   5.____

6. In a biology demonstration, sterile petri dishes are exposed. One dish is left unexposed in order to
   A. reduce the cost of the demonstration
   B. conserve materials
   C. have a control
   D. have a spare dish in the event of emergency

   6.____

7. Of the following, the one that is NOT used as a general stain is
   A. Lugol's solution
   B. methylene blue
   C. gentian violet
   D. Benedict's solution

   7.____

8. In sterilizing agar, an autoclave is heated to 15 pounds pressure for approximately
   A. 2 minutes
   B. 20 minutes
   C. 2 hours
   D. 20 hours

   8.____

9. A bell-jar model of the lungs can be made to demonstrate inhalation by _____ the rubber sheet.
   A. heating
   B. lowering
   C. piercing
   D. raising

   9.____

10. Three substances found in gastric juices are
    A. H_2O, pepsin, HCl
    B. H_2O, pepsin, H_2SO_4
    C. H_2O, ptyalin, HCl
    D. H_2O, ptyalin, H_2O, H_2SO_4

    10.____

11. Emulsification of fat in the intestine is aided by a liquid called
    A. chime B. chyle C. bile D. lacteal

12. In demonstrating the presence of starch in floods, the one substance that would NOT be suitable is
    A. eggplant B. asparagus C. macaroni D. potato

13. In a demonstration of photosynthesis, one leaf of a geranium plant is covered with black paper in order to
    A. protect the leaf from injury
    B. show the importance of light
    C. transmit monochromatic light
    D. show that the plant is healthy

14. Digestion of starch in a test tube can be demonstrated by adding
    A. albumin
    B. glucose
    C. artificial gastric juice
    D. saliva

15. Capillary circulation of blood may be demonstrated readily by using a
    A. white rat's tail
    B. goldfish tail
    C. drosophila fly's wing
    D. lens of a frog's eye

16. Plants that are kept under a bell jar
    A. need extra minerals
    B. need additional oxygen
    C. do not need to be watered frequently
    D. shrink in size

17. In the laboratory, live frogs are BEST kept in health condition by housing them in
    A. a moist chamber
    B. a hot-air oven
    C. agar agar solution
    D. an autoclave

18. In testing for the presence of simple sugar, one should use
    A. ACTH
    B. Benedict's solution
    C. isotonic solution
    D. cortisone

19. The movement of protozoa on a microscope slide may be slowed down satisfactorily by using
    A. Duco cement
    B. ammonia solution
    C. strong salt solution
    D. teased lens paper

20. Among angiosperms, the male gametophytes are MOST closely associated with
    A. carpels B. the nucellus C. pollen grains D. sporophylls

21. Of the following, the one with the MOST dominant sporophyte generation is
    A. spirogyra
    B. the bird moss
    C. the Christmas fern
    D. the white pine

22. The part of the microscope that controls the amount of entering light is called the
    A. diaphragm   B. eyepiece   C. nosepiece   D. stage

23. The gland that controls the other ductless glands in the body is the
    A. adrenal   B. parathyroid   C. pituitary   D. thyroid

24. Even after being blown over on its side, a plant will grow upward. This is an example of behavior known as
    A. negative geotropism   B. negative heliotropism
    C. positive geotropism   D. a reflex act

25. The scientist who experimented with conditioned reflexes was
    A. von Behring   B. Hooke   C. Pavlov   D. Lamarck

KEY (CORRECT ANSWERS)

1. C
2. A
3. C
4. C
5. B

6. C
7. D
8. B
9. B
10. A

11. C
12. B
13. B
14. D
15. B

16. C
17. A
18. B
19. D
20. C

21. D
22. A
23. C
24. A
25. C

TEST 4

DIRECTIONS: Each question or incomplete statement is followed by several suggested answers or completions. Select the one that BEST answers the question or completes the statement. *PRINT THE LETTER OF THE CORRECT ANSWER IN THE SPACE AT THE RIGHT.*

1. Three of the following behaviors are examples of reflex acts. The one that is NOT is
    A. blinking   B. sneezing   C. swallowing   D. whistling

    1._____

2. When red and white four o'clock flowers are cross-pollinated, the resulting flowers are
    A. pink   B. variegated   C. red   D. white

    2._____

3. The beating heart of a dissected frog may be kept alive by keeping it moistened with _____ solution.
    A. Ringer's   B. hypotonic   C. Fehling's   D. hypo

    3._____

4. Of the following, the one that is NOT classified as an enzyme is
    A. erepsin   B. pepsin   C. paracutin   D. trypsin

    4._____

5. The prehistoric man MOST closely resembling present-day man is thought to be the _____ man.
    A. Cro-Magnon   B. Java   C. Neanderthal   D. Peking

    5._____

6. Cardiac muscle is found only in the
    A. alimentary tract   B. heart
    C. intestinal wall   D. lower dermis

    6._____

7. The brontosaurus was MOST closely related to our present
    A. frog   B. salamander   C. snake   D. porpoise

    7._____

8. Of the following, the substance that is NOT a member of the vitamin B-complex is
    A. niacin   B. rennin   C. riboflavin   D. thiamin

    8._____

9. Scurvy is a disease caused by a deficiency in
    A. ascorbic acid   B. folic acid   C. vitamin A   D. vitamin K

    9._____

10. Bile is manufactured in the
    A. pancreas   B. liver   C. bile duct   D. spleen

    10._____

11. The diffusion of digested foods through the wall of the small intestine is known as
    A. absorption   B. digestion   C. katabolism   D. excretion

    11._____

12. "Rh positive" is an expression
    A. denoting a blood type
    B. denoting radioactive isotopes
    C. indicating the presence of syphilis
    D. indicating the presence of a tumor

13. When blood leaves the right side of the human heart, it goes to the
    A. vena cava   B. head   C. lungs   D. aorta

14. Blood vessels that have valves are termed
    A. arteries   B. carterioles   C. capillaries   D. veins

15. A bean plant is grown in a box which has an opening at one end. The purpose of this is to demonstrate
    A. positive phototropism
    B. negative hydrotropism
    C. negative phototropism
    D. positive hydrotropism

16. The order through which air passes into the body after entering the nostrils is
    A. windpipe, larynx, bronchi, air sacs
    B. larynx, bronchi, windpipe, air sacs
    C. larynx, windpipe, bronchi, air sacs
    D. air sacs, larynx, windpipe, bronchi

17. The President's illness in 1956 resulted from an inflammation of that portion of the small intestine called the
    A. ascending colon
    B. duodenum
    C. ileum
    D. jejenum

18. The vitamin essential for the proper clotting of blood is vitamin
    A. A   B. B_{12} C. C   D. K

19. The cambium layer in a tree is important because it provides for
    A. anchorage
    B. growth
    C. passage of materials
    D. protection

20. The structure which is a mature ovary together with associated flower parts is the
    A. calyx   B. fruit   C. seed   D. ovule

21. Of the following animals, the one possessing marked variable temperature is the
    A. snake   B. elephant   C. horse   D. canary

22. Of the following, the BEST rooting medium for cuttings is
    A. clean, sharp sand
    B. humus
    C. potting soil
    D. vermiculite

23. The branching habit of a tree may be learned MOST readily from the position of the
    A. axillary buds
    B. lenticels
    C. terminal buds
    D. terminal bud scale scars

23._____

24. An egg-laying mammal is the
    A. kangaroo
    B. lemur
    C. oppossum
    D. platypus

24._____

25. Birds possess great buoyancy because their respiratory system is connected with the system called
    A. circulatory
    B. digestive
    C. excretory
    D. skeletal

25._____

KEY (CORRECT ANSWERS)

1.	D	11.	A
2.	A	12.	A
3.	A	13.	C
4.	C	14.	D
5.	A	15.	A
6.	B	16.	C
7.	C	17.	C
8.	B	18.	D
9.	A	19.	B
10.	B	20.	B

21. A
22. D
23. A
24. D
25. D

TEST 5

DIRECTIONS: Each question or incomplete statement is followed by several suggested answers or completions. Select the one that BEST answers the question or completes the statement. *PRINT THE LETTER OF THE CORRECT ANSWER IN THE SPACE AT THE RIGHT.*

1. In order to keep the soil of a terrarium from souring, it is advisable to add 1.____
    A. a large quantity of water B. charcoal
    C. only potting soil D. sand

2. The MOST frequent cause of cloudy water and polluted aquaria is 2.____
    A. dirty gravel B. diseased plants
    C. over-feeding D. sick fish

3. Materials can be exchanged readily through the walls of 3.____
    A. arteries and capillaries B. arteries and veins
    C. capillaries alone D. veins and capillaries

4. Cell bodies of sensory neurons lie in the 4.____
    A. blind spot B. dorsal root C. frontal lobe D. ventral root

5. The autonomic nervous system controls 5.____
    A. blood pressure B. peristalsis
    C. sweating D. all of the above

6. A muscle fiber contracts 6.____
    A. either maximally or not at all
    B. in proportion to the innervation
    C. in relation to the contraction of other muscle fibers
    D. only when ATP has been excreted

7. The rate of respiration is controlled by the 7.____
    A. decrease of oxygen in the blood stream
    B. respiratory center in the medulla
    C. motor area in the cerebral cortex
    D. inhibiting action of the phrenic nerve

8. The glomerulus is a functioning unit in the 8.____
    A. kidney B. skin C. lung D. liver

9. Amebae accomplish ingestion by means of 9.____
    A. chelipeds B. oral grooves
    C. pseudopods D. tentacles

10. Auxin is to the plant as which one of the following is to the animal? 10.____
    A. Pepsin B. Ptyalin C. Rennin D. Thyroxin

11. To kill all bacteria in milk, it is necessary to
    A. dialyze   B. sterilize   C. pasteurize   D. homogenize

12. Peristalsis is MOST characteristic of the
    A. arteries   B. intestines   C. kidneys   D. liver

13. The energy release in the body depends upon enzyme systems which store energy in the form of the high energy bonds of
    A. ACTH   B. ATP   C. DDT   D. 2, 4D

14. There is no flow of blood from the aorta back into the heart because of the action of the
    A. bicuspid valve   B. mitral valve
    C. semi-lunar valves   D. tricuspid valve

15. The incorporation of amino acids into body protoplasm is termed
    A. absorption   B. assimilation
    C. deamination   D. digestion

16. ACTH, used in the treatment of arthritis, is derived from the
    A. adrenal   B. pancreas   C. pituitary   D. thyroid

17. Of the following materials, the one NOT classified as an antibiotic is
    A. aureomycin   B. V-penicillin
    C. terramycin   D. chromatin

18. Immediate immunity for a child exposed to diphtheria can be provided by
    A. antitoxin   B. toxin
    C. toxin-antitoxin   D. toxoid

19. Of the following, the only living disease agents that have been crystallized are the
    A. proteins   B. rickettsiae   C. spirochetes   D. viruses

20. In the following sequences, the one CORRECT sequence is
    A. cleavage, fertilization, gastrulation, metamorphosis, larva
    B. cleavage, fertilization, metamorphosis, gastrulation, larva
    C. fertilization, cleavage, gastrulation, larva, metamorphosis
    D. fertilization, gastrulation, cleavage, larva, metamorphosis

21. To distinguish a heterozygous black guinea pig from a homozygous black one
    A. examine its physical features carefully
    B. mate it with a heterozygous black
    C. mate it with a homozygous black
    D. mate it with a white

22. A 9:3:3:1 ratio is obtained in a _____ cross involving _____ dominance.   22.____
    A. dihybrid; complete   B. dihybrid; incomplete
    C. monohybrid; complete   D. monohybrid; incomplete

23. Three of the following terms are properly grouped together. The one which   23.____
    does NOT belong is
    A. allantois   B. amnion   C. chorion   D. fovea

24. All genes lying on the same chromosome are said to be   24.____
    A. crossed over   B. independently assorted
    C. linked   D. segregated

25. Of the following scientists, three are associated with the same type of inquiry.   25.____
    The scientist who does NOT belong in the group is
    A. Darwin   B. Lamarck   C. Lysenko   D. Schwann

KEY (CORRECT ANSWERS)

1.	B	11.	B
2.	C	12.	B
3.	C	13.	B
4.	B	14.	C
5.	D	15.	B
6.	A	16.	C
7.	B	17.	D
8.	A	18.	A
9.	C	19.	D
10.	D	20.	C

21. D
22. A
23. D
24. C
25. D

EXAMINATION SECTION
TEST 1

DIRECTIONS: Each question or incomplete statement is followed by several suggested answers or completions. Select the one that BEST answers the question or completes the statement. *PRINT THE LETTER OF THE CORRECT ANSWER IN THE SPACE AT THE RIGHT.*

1. One liter is *approximately* one
   A. gallon B. gill C. pint D. quart

   1.____

2. The color of freshly prepared *cleaning solution* is
   A. black B. blue C. green D. red

   2.____

3. *Cleaning solution* is GENERALLY prepared by pouring the
   A. aqueous solution of sodium dichromate into the concentrated sulfuric acid
   B. concentrated sulfuric acid into the aqueous solution of sodium dichromate
   C. concentrated hydrochloric acid into the concentrated nitric acid
   D. concentrated nitric acid into the concentrated hydrochloric acid s

   3.____

4. Commercial formalin is *approximately* _____ formaldehyde.
   A. 20% B. 40% C. 66% D. 80%

   4.____

5. In microscopy, the optical tube length is *approximately* 16
   A. cm B. km C. m D. mm

   5.____

6. The magnifying power of the oil-immersion objective is *approximately*
   A. 10 B. 45 C. 95 D. 215

   6.____

7. The high power dry lens of the compound microscope is the _____ objective.
   A. 1.8-mm B. 4-mm C. 8-mm D. 16-mm

   7.____

8. The focal length of the *oil-immersion* lens is *approximately* _____ mm.
   A. 2 B. 4 C. 8 D. 16

   8.____

9. In microscopic work, the magnification obtained by using the 16-mm objective and a 10x ocular is *approximately*
   A. 40 B. 100 C. 160 D. 200

   9.____

10. One micron is equal to _____ cm.
    A. 10^{-2} B. 10^{-3} C. 10^{-4} D. 10^{-5}

    10.____

11. Cedar oil used in microscopic work has ESSENTIALLY the same index of refraction as
    A. acetone B. air C. glass D. water

    11.____

12. The saturated calomel electrode is GENERALLY used as the reference electrode for measuring
    A. light intensity B. pH
    C. temperature D. turbidity

13. The use of the comparator block in determining the reaction of culture media is a _____ method.
    A. calorimetric B. colorimetric
    C. electrometric D. gasometric

14. The pH value for a neutral solution is
    A. 6 B. 7 C. 8 D. 9

15. A pH of 6 means that the [H⁺] is equal to
    A. 0.6 B. 6 C. 10^6 D. 10^{-6}

16. The pH of a solution containing 0.0001 grams of hydrogen ions per liter is
    A. 3 B. 4 C. 5 D. 6

17. Of the following filters, the one made from diatomaceous earth is the
    A. Berkefeld B. Chamberland C. Elford D. Seitz

18. The substance GENERALLY used to prevent foaming during a bacteriological type of laboratory filtration is
    A. acetic acid B. caprylic alcohol
    C. sodium bicarbonate D. sodium chloride

19. The pressure GENERALLY recommended for carrying out a bacteriological type of laboratory filtration is approximately _____ cm Hg.
    A. 30 B. 60 C. 90 D. 120

20. The retentive property of a filter is GENERALLY tested by using a culture of
    A. Aerobacter aerogenes B. Bacillus subtilis
    C. Escherichia coli D. Serratin marcescens

21. Ultrafilters used in the study of ultramicroscopic viruses are GENERALLY made from
    A. asbestos B. collodion
    C. diatomaceous earth D. porcelain

22. The term *quebec* is GENERALLY associated with a type of
    A. autoclave B. colony counter
    C. colorimeter D. microscope

23. The term *whipple* refers to a type of
    A. media B. micrometer
    C. sterilizer D. test tube

24. Of the following indicators, the one with a pH range of *approximately* 6.0 - 7.6 is   24._____

    A. brom thymol blue   B. cresol red
    C. phenol red   D. thymol blue

25. The pH range of phenolphthalein is *approximately*   25._____

    A. 2.9 - 4.0   B. 5.1 - 6.7   C. 7.0 - 8.6   D. 8.3 - 10.0

KEY (CORRECT ANSWERS)

1.	D	11.	C
2.	D	12.	B
3.	B	13.	B
4.	B	14.	B
5.	A	15.	D
6.	C	16.	B
7.	B	17.	A
8.	A	18.	B
9.	B	19.	A
10.	C	20.	D

21. B
22. B
23. B
24. A
25. D

TEST 2

DIRECTIONS: Each question or incomplete statement is followed by several suggested answers or completions. Select the one that BEST answers the question or completes the statement. *PRINT THE LETTER OF THE CORRECT ANSWER IN THE SPACE AT THE RIGHT.*

1. The color of brom thymol blue indicator on the alkaline side of its pH range is   1.____
   A. blue   B. colorless   C. red   D. yellow

2. The color of phenol red indicator on the acid side of its pH range is   2.____
   A. blue   B. colorless   C. red   D. yellow

3. Of the following, the one FREQUENTLY used as a counter-stain in the Gram staining technique is   3.____
   A. ammonium oxalate   B. crystal violet
   C. iodine   D. safranin

4. Lugol's solution is used in the Gram stain as a   4.____
   A. counterstain   B. decolorizer
   C. mordant   D. primary stain

5. The Hucker modification is GENERALLY associated with the _____ stain.   5.____
   A. acid-fast   B. capsule   C. Gram   D. spore

6. The method GENERALLY associated with staining for capsules is the   6.____
   A. Dorner   B. Hiss   C. Neisser   D. Seller

7. The Ziehl-Neelsen method is GENERALLY associated with the _____ stain.   7.____
   A. acid-fast   B. capsule   C. Gram   D. flagella

8. The method GENERALLY associated with staining for spores is the   8.____
   A. Castaneda   B. Dorner   C. Kopeloff   D. Pappenheim

9. The method GENERALLY associated with staining for flagella is the   9.____
   A. Huntoon   B. Loeffler   C. Machiavello   D. Stettinius

10. The genus Mycobacterium is classified with the   10.____
    A. Actinomycetales   B. Eubacteriales
    C. Rickettsiales   D. Spirochaetales

11. Endospore formation is a distinguishing feature of organisms belonging to the   11.____
    A. Bacillaceae   B. Micrococcaceae
    C. Neisseriaceae   D. Spirochaetaceae

12. In microbiological taxonomy, an *-eae* ending indicates   12.____
    A. class   B. family   C. order   D. tribe

13. Bacteriophage may be used for the typing of organisms causing   13.____

    A. bacillary dysentery   B. cholera
    C. gonorrhea   D. typhoid fever

14. The term M.P.N. is used to   14.____

    A. determine motility of organisms
    B. differentiate between *fecal* and *non-fecal* types
    C. estimate the coliform group density
    D. prepare culture media

15. The carbohydrate GENERALLY found in the test medium used for the methyl red test is   15.____

    A. dextrose   B. lactose   C. maltose   D. sucrose

Questions 16-25.

DIRECTIONS: Column I lists the specific names of pathogens, each of which is to be matched with one of the generic names given in Column II. For each item of Column I, write the letter in front of the generic option in Column II which completes the scientific name of the microorganism, based upon current nomenclature.

Column I

16. Anthracis
17. Comma
18. Diphthariae
19. Ducreyi
20. Dysenteriae
21. Leprae
22. Pairidum
23. Suis
24. Tetani
25. Vulgaris

Column II

A. Actinobacillus
B. Bacillus
C. Borrelia
D. Brucella
E. Clostridium
F. Corynebacterium
G. Hemophilus
H. Leptospira
I. Malleomyces
J. Mycobacterium
K. Pasteurella
L. Proteus
M. Shigella
N. Treponema
O. Vibrio

16.____
17.____
18.____
19.____
20.____
21.____
22.____
23.____
24.____
25.____

KEY (CORRECT ANSWERS)

1. A
2. D
3. D
4. C
5. C

6. B
7. A
8. B
9. B
10. A

11. A
12. D
13. D
14. C
15. A

16. B
17. O
18. F
19. G
20. M

21. J
22. N
23. D
24. E
25. L

EXAMINATION SECTION
TEST 1

DIRECTIONS: Each question or incomplete statement is followed by several suggested answers or completions. Select the one that BEST answers the question or completes the statement. *PRINT THE LETTER OF THE CORRECT ANSWER IN THE SPACE AT THE RIGHT.*

1. The boiling point of water at 1 atmosphere pressure is 100 on the _____ scale.   1._____

   A. Baumé B. Centigrade
   C. Fahrenheit D. Kelvin

2. Ordinary atmospheric pressure on a mercury barometer is 76   2._____

   A. centimeters B. inches
   C. feet D. millimeters

3. The density of water is MOST NEARLY one   3._____

   A. gram per square centimeter
   B. kilogram per liter
   C. pound per quart
   D. pound per square inch

4. A round-bottomed flask is also called a _____ flask.   4._____

   A. boiling B. Claisen
   C. Erlenmeyer D. volumetric

5. The term *Buchner* refers to a type of   5._____

   A. condenser B. crucible C. funnel D. tube

6. The term *Westphal* refers to a type of   6._____

   A. balance B. burner C. condenser D. flask

7. The term *Nessler* refers to a type of   7._____

   A. balance B. flask
   C. hydrometer D. tube

8. Of the following, the one used to determine the freezing point of liquids is the   8._____

   A. calorimeter B. cryoscope
   C. polariscope D. pyenometer

9. Of the following, the one which is the DENSEST liquid is   9._____

   A. alcohol B. benzene
   C. water D. carbon tetrachloride

10. A Kipp generator is *generally* used to generate   10._____

    A. alternating current B. direct current
    C. helium gas D. hydrogen sulfide

39

11. The one of the following gases which is LIGHTER than air is   11.____

    A. ammonia   B. bromine
    C. carbon dioxide   D. oxygen

12. Of the following halogens, the one which has the LOWEST atomic weight is   12.____

    A. bromine   B. chlorine   C. fluorine   D. iodine

13. Small amounts of sodium left unreacted in the bottom of a flask are *generally* destroyed by   13.____

    A. adding absolute alcohol   B. adding boiling water
    C. adding hot benzene   D. heating to dull redness

14. The color of freshly prepared *cleaning solution* is   14.____

    A. blue   B. green   C. red   D. yellow

15. To assure delivery of the proper volume, a pipette marked *25 ml (Deliver)* should be allowed to empty,   15.____

    A. and then be immediately removed from the receiving vessel
    B. and then the last few drops should be blown out
    C. drained for 30 seconds, and then the last few drops should be blown out
    D. drained for 30 seconds, and then touched to the wall of the receiving vessel

16. The SAFEST way to heat a distilling flask containing ether is with a(n)   16.____

    A. electrical heater or hot plate
    B. oxygen-gas burner
    C. small Bunsen flame
    D. Wood's metal bath

17. Of the following laboratory procedures, the one which is MOST dangerous is adding   17.____

    A. alcohol to water
    B. concentrated sulfuric acid to water
    C. water to alcohol
    D. water to concentrated sulfuric acid

18. If $x^2 = 10^{-14}$, then $x =$ 18.____

    A. 10^{-7} B. 10^{-12} C. 10^{-16} D. 10^{-28}

19. The normality of a solution of 0.10 molar acetic acid _____ normality of a 0.10 molar solution of HCl.   19.____

    A. bears no relation to the
    B. is higher than the
    C. is lower than the
    D. is the same as the

20. The average weighing error on the standard analytical balance is MOST NEARLY   20.____

    A. 0.02 grams   B. 0.2 grams
    C. 0.2 milligrams   D. 2 micrograms

21. The amount of 0.20 N NaOH which will EXACTLY neutralize 20 ml of 0.10 N HCl is _____ ml.

    A. 5   B. 10   C. 20   D. 40

22. Of the following, the one which is LEAST reactive is

    A. argon   B. chlorine   C. hydrogen   D. nitrogen

23. Of the following, the one which is a STRONG oxidizing agent is

    A. argon   B. chlorine   C. hydrogen   D. nitrogen

24. Of the following metals, the one with the LOWEST density is

    A. aluminum   B. copper   C. iron   D. zinc

25. A weighted sample of an unknown metal is dissolved in dilute acid and the volume of evolved hydrogen, dried and reduced to STP is determined.
    This information is *sufficient* to determine the metal's

    A. atomic number   B. atomic weight
    C. equivalent weight   D. molecular weight

KEY (CORRECT ANSWERS)

1. B		11. A	
2. A		12. C	
3. B		13. A	
4. A		14. C	
5. C		15. D	
6. A		16. A	
7. D		17. D	
8. B		18. A	
9. D		19. D	
10. D		20. C	

21. B
22. A
23. B
24. A
25. C

TEST 2

DIRECTIONS: Each question or incomplete statement is followed by several suggested answers or completions. Select the one that BEST answers the question or completes the statement. *PRINT THE LETTER OF THE CORRECT ANSWER IN THE SPACE AT THE RIGHT.*

1. The weight percent of hydrogen in water is MOST NEARLY 1.____
   A. 5.9 B. 11.1 C. 33.3 D. 50.0

2. Of the following, the instrument used to measure the density of an unknown liquid is the 2.____
   A. ebullioscope B. polarimeter
   C. pycnometer D. viscosimeter

3. Of the following, the one which is an indicator *commonly* used in acid-base titrations is 3.____
   A. indigo
   B. methyl red
   C. silver chromate
   D. tetramethyl ammonium chloride

4. A solution of one mole of cane sugar in 1000 gms of water 4.____
   A. freezes at a higher temperature than pure water
   B. freezes at a lower temperature than pure water
   C. freezes at the same temperature as pure water
   D. will not freeze at all

5. The vacuum bottle or thermos bottle is also called the _____ flask. 5.____
   A. Dewar B. Erlenmeyer
   C. Florence D. Wolff

6. The gram-molecular weight of hydrogen gas is _____ gms. 6.____
   A. 0.0084 B. 1.008 C. 2.016 D. 22.4

7. An electron has a 7.____
   A. charge depending on the atomic number
   B. negative charge
   C. positive charge
   D. zero charge

8. Elements with the same atomic number but different atomic weights are called 8.____
   A. isentropes B. isobars
   C. isomers D. isotopes

9. A mole of helium gas has a volume, at standard temperature and pressure, of _____ liter(s). 9.____
   A. 1 B. 11.2 C. 22.4 D. 44.8

10. If 100 ml of a gas at standard temperature and pressure is changed to a pressure of 1520 mm Hg and a temperature of 273° C, its volume

    A. is changed to 50 ml
    B. is changed to 200 ml
    C. is changed to 400 ml
    D. remains unchanged

10.____

11. The extraction of I_2 from 100 ml of a water solution is performed MOST efficiently by

    A. one 50-ml portion of CCl_4
    B. one 50-ml portion of ethanol
    C. five 10-ml portions of CCl_4
    D. five 10-ml portions of ethanol

11.____

12. The RECOMMENDED way of making a U-shaped bend in 8 mm soft glass tubing is

    A. by wrapping with nichrome wire and heating electrically
    B. in a Bunsen flame
    C. in an acetylene-oxygen blast lamp
    D. in an oxyhydrogen blast lamp

12.____

13. Fire-polishing removes

    A. cloudiness from devitrified glass
    B. etching from the bottom of flasks and beakers
    C. rough edges from glass tubing
    D. scratches and abrasions from glass

13.____

14. One inch is APPROXIMATELY _____ mm.

    A. 0.025   B. 0.25   C. 2.5   D. 25

14.____

15. One liter is APPROXIMATELY

    A. 1 pint   B. 1 quart   C. 2 quarts   D. 1 gallon

15.____

16. Of the following gases, the ONLY one which can be collected by the upward displacement of air is

    A. CO_2 B. H_2 C. NO_2 D. SO_2

16.____

17. Of the following gases, the one which is MOST poisonous is

    A. CO_2 B. H_2 C. H_2S D. N_2O

17.____

18. Of the following gases, the one which has a noticeable color is

    A. NH_3 B. NO   C. NO_2 D. N_2O

18.____

19. Of the following, the one with the HIGHEST boiling point is

    A. HCl   B. HNO_3 C. H_2O D. H_2SO_4

19.____

20. Of the following, the one with the HIGHEST melting point is

    A. acetone   B. hydrogen   C. mercury   D. water

20.____

21. pH is defined as the   21._____

    A. [H⁺]   B. log [H⁺]   C. -log [H⁺]   D. log (10[H⁺])

22. A Wheatstone bridge is used for   22._____

    A. connecting glass to rubber
    B. holding a funnel over a beaker
    C. measuring hardness
    D. measuring electrical resistances

23. Of the following substances, the one which is MOST inflammable is   23._____

    A. CCl_4 B. $CHCl_3$ C. Cl_2 D. Na_2CO_3

24. One pound is APPROXIMATELY _____ grams.   24._____

    A. 0.065   B. 28.3   C. 454   D. 1000

25. A catalyst is a substance which   25._____

    A. changes the point of equilibrium of a reaction
    B. increases the dissociation of weak acids
    C. increases the rate of a reaction
    D. reacts with undesired products of a reaction

KEY (CORRECT ANSWERS)

1. B
2. C
3. B
4. B
5. A

6. C
7. B
8. D
9. C
10. D

11. C
12. B
13. C
14. D
15. B

16. B
17. C
18. C
19. D
20. D

21. C
22. D
23. B
24. C
25. C

EXAMINATION SECTION
TEST 1

DIRECTIONS: Each question or incomplete statement is followed by several suggested answers or completions. Select the one that BEST answers the question or completes the statement. *PRINT THE LETTER OF THE CORRECT ANSWER IN THE SPACE AT THE RIGHT.*

1. The part of the compound microscope on which the slide is placed is called the   1.____
   A. base   B. condenser   C. diaphragm   D. stage

2. The part of an analytical balance which supports the arms is called the   2.____
   A. beam
   C. rest point
   B. pointer
   D. spirit level

3. Hematocrit can be determined by packing the red cells in a blood sample with a(n)   3.____
   A. centrifuge
   C. extractor
   B. condenser
   D. pipetting machine

4. The instrument used for measuring the pressure of liquids or gases is known as a   4.____
   A. calorimeter
   C. manometer
   B. colorimeter
   D. micrometer

5. Specific gravity can be measured with the   5.____
   A. homogenizer
   C. hygrometer
   B. hydrometer
   D. turbidometer

6. Steam under pressure is sometimes used to sterilize laboratory equipment. The apparatus used for this is called a(n)   6.____
   A. hot air oven
   C. Arnold sterilizer
   B. pyrometer
   D. autoclave

7. When using an analytical balance, the balance case should be closed while final adjustments are made.
   This is done to prevent errors from   7.____
   A. air currents
   C. humidity
   B. dust
   D. static electricity

8. The one of the following pieces of laboratory equipment which is subject to *strike back* is the   8.____
   A. analytical balance
   C. bunsen burner
   B. Berkefeld filter
   D. simple microscope

9. For ordinary laboratory purposes, the FINAL step in cleaning glassware should be a rinse in   9.____
   A. chromic acid
   C. ethyl alcohol
   B. distilled water
   D. trisodium phosphate

10. The one of the following that is GENERALLY sterilized with a flame is a

    A. filter   B. pipette   C. slide   D. test tube

11. A microtome is GENERALLY used to

    A. distill water
    B. record sounds
    C. section tissue
    D. weigh small objects

12. When labels are placed on glass slides, the labels can be protected by painting with

    A. ethylene glycol
    B. glycerol
    C. melted paraffin
    D. petroleum ether

13. All of the following oils may be used with an oil-immersion objective EXCEPT _____ oil.

    A. cedarwood   B. immersion   C. machine   D. mineral

14. The purpose of the coarse adjuster of a compound microscope is to

    A. adjust the intensity of the light
    B. move the stage so that the area to be examined is beneath the objective
    C. obtain approximate focus
    D. obtain exact focus

15. The magnification of any combination of objectives and oculars may be obtained by _____ the magnification of the

    A. adding; ocular
    B. multiplying; ocular
    C. subtracting; ocular
    D. subtracting; objective

16. The purpose of the mirror on a compound microscope is to

    A. direct light downward through the ocular
    B. direct light upward through the condenser
    C. reflect light away from the stage
    D. reflect the image onto a screen

17. In some laboratories, file folders borrowed by technicians from other laboratories are returned to a central location to be refiled by a technician from that laboratory. This practice is

    A. *desirable;* to prevent misfiling, only technicians who know the filing system should refile material
    B. *undesirable;* this creates extra work for laboratory personnel
    C. *desirable;* technicians from other laboratories might come across confidential information in the files
    D. *undesirable;* folders should be returned to the files immediately in case others want to use them

18. If small documents must be filed in standard size file folders, the BEST way to prevent them from becoming lost or damaged is to

    A. fasten them to the cover of the folder
    B. glue them to standard-size paper
    C. place them neatly in the back of the folder
    D. staple them together and place them in the front of the folder

19. 1,000,000 may be represented as 19.____

   A. 10^3 B. 10^5 C. 10^6 D. 10^{10}

20. 35° Centigrade equals 20.____

   A. 70° F B. 95° F C. 100° F D. 120° F

21. $10^3 \times 10^4$ equals 21.____

   A. 10^7 B. 10^{12} C. 100^7 D. 100^{12}

22. If a mixture is made up of one part Substance A, 3 parts Substance B, and 12 parts Substance C, the proportion of Substance A in the mixture is 22.____

   A. 4% B. 6 1/4% C. 16% D. 62 1/2%

23. If 5 grams of a chemical are enough to perform a certain laboratory test 9 times, the quantity of the chemical needed to perform this test 1,350 times would be _____ grams. 23.____

   A. 30 B. 150 C. 270 D. 750

24. If it takes 7 grams of a certain substance to make 5 liters of a solution, the quantity of the substance needed to make 4 liters of the solution is _____ grams. 24.____

   A. 2.85 B. 4.70 C. 5.60 D. 8.75

25. If it takes 3 grams of Substance A and 7 grams of Substance B to make 4 liters of a solution, how many grams of Substances A and B does it take to make 5 liters of the solution? 25.____
   _____ of Substance A and of Substance B.

   A. 3.35; 6.65 B. 3.50; 7.50
   C. 3.75; 8.75 D. 4; 7

26. A certain type of laboratory test can be performed by a laboratory technician in 20 minutes. 26.____
   Three laboratory technicians can perform 243 such tests in _____ hours.

   A. 16 B. 20 C. 27 D. 81

27. Pairs of shatterproof plastic safety glasses cost $3.80 each, but an 8% discount is given on orders of six pairs or more. Pairs of straight blade dissecting scissors cost $14.40 a dozen with a 12% discount on orders of two dozen or more. 27.____
   The total cost of eight pairs of safety glasses and 30 pairs of dissecting scissors is MOST NEARLY

   A. $59.65 B. $62.10 C. $66.40 D. $73.15

28. On July 1, your laboratory has 280 usable 20-gauge needles on hand. On August 1, 15% of these needles have been lost or damaged beyond repair. On August 15, a new shipment of 50 needles is received by the laboratory, but 10% of these arrive damaged and are returned to the seller. 28.____
   At this point, the number of usable 20-gauge needles on hand would be

   A. 238 B. 283 C. 288 D. 325

29. A certain laboratory procedure can be completed by a laboratory technician in 15 minutes.
    If your lab is assigned 30 such tests, and they must be completed within 3 hours, the MINIMUM number of technicians that would have to be assigned to this task is

    A. 2   B. 3   C. 4   D. 5

30. An endothermic reaction is one in which

    A. the boiling point is raised
    B. the boiling point is lowered
    C. heat is liberated
    D. heat is absorbed

31. A substance which increases the rate of a chemical reaction is termed a(n)

    A. isotope B. polymer C. catalyst D. hydrate

32. The process of converting a solid into a liquid by means of heat is called

    A. incineration   B. fusion
    C. distillation   D. carbonization

33. The valence of the nitrate (NO_3) radical is

    A. 0   B. -1   C. -2   D. -3

34. The chemical name for wood alcohol is

    A. methanol   B. ethanol
    C. butanol   D. absolute alcohol

35. The molecular weight of hydrogen is MOST NEARLY

    A. 1   B. 2   C. 14   D. 16

36. In a laboratory filtration, the solid left on the filter paper is USUALLY called the

    A. distillate   B. filtrate
    C. precipitate   D. solute

Questions 37-40.

DIRECTIONS: Questions 37 through 40 pertain to the meaning of terms which may be encountered in laboratory work. For each question, select the option whose meaning is MOST NEARLY the same as that of the numbered item.

37. atrophied

    A. enlarged   B. relaxed
    C. strengthened   D. wasted

38. leucocyte

    A. white cell   B. red cell
    C. epithelial cell   D. dermal cell

39. permeable

    A. volatile   B. variable
    C. flexible   D. penetrable

39.____

40. attenuate

    A. dilute   B. infect
    C. oxidize   D. strengthen

40.____

KEY (CORRECT ANSWERS)

1. D	11. C	21. A	31. C
2. A	12. C	22. B	32. B
3. A	13. C	23. D	33. B
4. C	14. C	24. C	34. A
5. B	15. B	25. C	35. B
6. D	16. B	26. C	36. C
7. A	17. A	27. A	37. D
8. C	18. B	28. B	38. A
9. B	19. C	29. B	39. D
10. C	20. B	30. D	40. A

TEST 2

DIRECTIONS: Each question or incomplete statement is followed by several suggested answers or completions. Select the one that BEST answers the question or completes the statement. *PRINT THE LETTER OF THE CORRECT ANSWER IN THE SPACE AT THE RIGHT.*

1. Assume that there are six laboratory technicians working in a certain laboratory. Four of them are well-trained, efficient workers and can perform a certain procedure in 15 minutes. The other two are newly-hired and have not completed their training. It takes each of them twice as long to perform that procedure.
   If all six are assigned to perform 70 such procedures, they can complete the work in _____ hours.

   A. 3   B. 3 1/2   C. 4   D. 4 1/2

2. Inoculation under the skin is termed

   A. subdural   B. subcutaneous
   C. per os   D. sublingual

3. The four major blood groups are GENERALLY designated as groups

   A. A, B, AB, O   B. A, B, C, Rh
   C. A, B, K, O   D. AB, K, Rh, O

4. In acid-fast staining, the acid-fast bacteria are stained

   A. red   B. green   C. brown   D. blue

5. The optimum temperature for the growth of most pathogenic bacteria is APPROXIMATELY

   A. 35 °C   B. 55 °C   C. 75 °C   D. 95 °C

6. You are about to draw blood from a patient who speaks with a heavy foreign accent. He becomes very upset and, speaking rapidly, tries to explain something to you. However, you cannot understand him.
   The BEST thing for you to do would be to

   A. ask the person to speak slowly and have him repeat what he is trying to communicate
   B. draw the blood but note on the lab request that the patient became upset
   C. explain to the patient that the test will not hurt him and then draw the blood
   D. omit the blood test since it is upsetting the patient

7. The number of red blood corpuscles in each cubic millimeter of normal adult human blood is within the range of

   A. 75,000 to 85,000   B. 600,000 to 800,000
   C. 4,000,000 to 6,000,000   D. 10,000,000 to 20,000,000

8. The presence of casts is determined in the microscopic examination of

   A. spinal fluid   B. blood
   C. urine   D. feces

9. Benedict's reagent is used in urine analysis to test for

   A. ammonia B. bile C. protein D. sugar

10. Bacteria GENERALLY reproduce by

    A. fusion
    C. conjugation
    B. spore formation
    D. binary fission

11. Ringworm is a disease caused by

    A. worms B. viruses C. molds D. bacteria

12. Bacteria which grow best in the presence of free oxygen are called

    A. thermophiles
    C. anaerobes
    B. mesophiles
    D. aerobes

13. Of the following organisms, those GENERALLY considered to be the smallest in size are the

    A. viruses
    C. molds
    B. rickettsiae
    D. bacteria

14. The Ziehl-Neelsen staining method is GENERALLY associated with the _____ stain.

    A. spore B. Gram C. capsule D. acid-fast

15. The acid-fast stain is GENERALLY associated with the diagnosis of

    A. diphtheria
    C. tuberculosis
    B. syphilis
    D. typhoid fever

16. The Schick test is used to determine susceptibility to

    A. typhoid fever
    C. pneumonia
    B. tetanus
    D. diphtheria

17. In the Gram method, the Gram positive bacteria are stained

    A. brown B. green C. violet D. yellow

18. The RECOMMENDED method for storing metallic sodium is

    A. in alcohol
    B. in a box in the refrigerator
    C. under kerosene
    D. under water

19. The BEST way to put out a chemical fire is to

    A. smother it with a cylinder of nitrogen
    B. flood it with water
    C. use a carbon dioxide fire extinguisher
    D. use a carbon tetrachloride fire extinguisher

3 (#2)

20. The one of the following chemicals which is very flammable and should NOT be exposed to any flames or sparks is 20.____

    A. carbon disulfide
    B. formaldehyde
    C. methylene chloride
    D. potassium iodide

21. Which of the following solutions should NOT be kept in an ordinary refrigerator? 21.____
    A(n) _____ solution of _____ .

    A. alcohol; gram stain
    B. chloroform; cholesterol
    C. water; ammonium nitrate
    D. ether; triglycerides

22. The process whereby crystals lose their water of crystallization on exposure to the atmosphere is termed 22.____

    A. sublimation
    B. efflorescence
    C. declination
    D. decantation

23. A substance used to increase the stability of a dispersion of one liquid in another is called a(n) 23.____

    A. buffer   B. catalyst   C. aerator   D. emulsifier

24. The RECOMMENDED method of disposing of volatile, flammable solvents is to 24.____

    A. burn them in a secluded place
    B. evaporate them on a steam bath in a hood
    C. pour them down the sink with a lot of water
    D. put them in a steel garbage can with a tight-fitting lid

Questions 25-34.

DIRECTIONS: The following is a list of patients who were referred by various clinics to the laboratory for tests. After each name is a patient identification number. Questions 25 through 34 are to be answered on the basis of the information contained in this list and the explanation accompanying it.

The first digit refers to the clinic which made the referral:
- 1 - Cardiac
- 2 - Renal
- 3 - Pediatrics
- 4 - Opthalmology
- 5 - Orthopedics
- 6 - Hematology
- 7 - Gynecology
- 8 - Neurology
- 9 - Gastroenterology

The second digit refers to the sex of the patient:
- 1 - male
- 2 - female

The third and fourth digits give the age of the patient.

The last two digits give the day of the month the laboratory tests were performed.

LABORATORY REFERRALS DURING JANUARY

Adams, Jacqueline	320917	Miller, Michael	111806
Black, Leslie	813406	Pratt, William	214411
Cook, Marie	511616	Rogers, Ellen	722428
Fisher, Pat	914625	Saunders, Sally	310229
Jackson, Lee	923212	Wilson, Jan	416715
James, Linda	624621	Wyatt, Mark	321326
Lane, Arthur	115702		

25. According to the list, the number of women referred to the laboratory during January was 25.____
    A. 4   B. 5   C. 6   D. 7

26. The clinic from which the MOST patients were referred was 26.____
    A. Cardiac   B. Gynecology   C. Opthamology   D. Pediatrics

27. The YOUNGEST patient referred from any clinic other than Pediatrics was 27.____
    A. Leslie Black
    B. Marie Cook
    C. Arthur Lane
    D. Sally Saunders

28. The number of patients whose laboratory tests were performed on or before January 21 was 28.____
    A. 7   B. 8   C. 9   D. 10

29. The number of patients referred for laboratory tests who are under age 45 is 29.____
    A. 7   B. 8   C. 9   D. 10

30. The OLDEST patient referred to the clinic during January was 30.____
    A. Jacqueline Adams
    B. Linda James
    C. Arthur Lane
    D. Jan Wilson

31. The ONLY patient treated in the Orthopedics clinic was 31.____
    A. Marie Cook
    B. Pat Fisher
    C. Ellen Rogers
    D. Jan Wilson

32. A woman age 37 was referred from the Hematology clinic to the laboratory. Her laboratory tests were performed on January 9.
    Her identification number would be 32.____
    A. 610937   B. 623709   C. 613790   D. 623790

33. A man was referred for lab tests from the Orthopedics clinic. He is 30 years old, and his tests were performed on January 6.
    His identification number would be 33.____
    A. 413006   B. 510360   C. 513006   D. 613060

34. A 4-year-old boy was referred from Pediatrics clinic to 34. _____
have laboratory tests on January 23. His identification number was

   A. 310422   B. 310423   C. 310433   D. 320403

Questions 35-38.

DIRECTIONS: Questions 35 through 38 are to be answered SOLELY on the basis of the information contained in the following table.

DEATH RATE FROM PULMONARY TUBERCULOSIS ACCORDING TO OCCUPATION (per 100,000 population) (County X, 1990)	
Unskilled workers	185
Semiskilled workers	102
Skilled workers and foremen	72
Clerks	66
Agricultural workers	47
Managers	43
Professionals	26

35. The occupation whose death rate was about one-fourth the death rate for semiskilled workers is

   A. agricultural workers   B. clerks
   C. managers   D. professionals

36. If 18% of the agricultural workers who died from pulmonary tuberculosis were women, out of 100,000 agricultural workers, the number of women who died from pulmonary tuberculosis is

   A. 3   B. 9   C. 18   D. 29

37. If there were 3,400,000 managers in County X in 1990, the number who died from pulmonary tuberculosis was

   A. 146   B. 1,151   C. 1,462   D. 1,849

38. Among the skilled workers and foremen who died from pulmonary tuberculosis in 1990, one-quarter had the expenses of their illness paid for entirely by insurance, and one-third had part of their medical expenses paid for by insurance.
Out of 100,000 skilled workers and foremen, the number who had all or part of their medical expenses paid for by insurance was MOST NEARLY

   A. 18   B. 24   C. 37   D. 42

39. Assume that one of your subordinates asks you for advice on a personal problem. The BEST thing for you to do would be to

   A. explain to the worker that personal problems should not be discussed during working hours
   B. have the worker transferred to a simple job where his preoccupation with his problem will not cause serious errors
   C. listen sympathetically to his story without telling him what to do about the problem
   D. tell the worker you will think over his problem and advise him the following day

40. Accuracy is extremely important in most laboratory work. If you find that a member of your staff has made several errors in the past few weeks, the BEST thing for you to do would be to

    A. ask him why he is being so careless
    B. discuss his inadequate performance at a meeting of your staff to see if they can suggest ways he can improve
    C. explain to him in private where his work in inaccurate and how he can improve it in the future
    D. threaten to give him a poor evaluation unless his work improves

40.____

KEY (CORRECT ANSWERS)

1.	B	11.	C	21.	D	31.	A
2.	B	12.	D	22.	B	32.	B
3.	A	13.	A	23.	D	33.	C
4.	A	14.	D	24.	B	34.	B
5.	A	15.	C	25.	B	35.	D
6.	A	16.	D	26.	D	36.	B
7.	C	17.	C	27.	B	37.	C
8.	C	18.	C	28.	C	38.	D
9.	D	19.	C	29.	C	39.	C
10.	D	20.	A	30.	D	40.	C

EXAMINATION SECTION
TEST 1

DIRECTIONS: Each question or incomplete statement is followed by several suggested answers or completions. Select the one that BEST answers the question or completes the statement. *PRINT THE LETTER OF THE CORRECT ANSWER IN THE SPACE AT THE RIGHT.*

1. After extensive use of the oil immersion lens of a compound microscope, xylol should be used to clean the

    A. condenser lens
    B. objective lens
    C. eyepiece
    D. iris diaphragm

    1._____

2. When using a compound microscope, it is necessary to focus light on the object by use of the

    A. condenser lens
    B. objective lens
    C. eyepiece
    D. iris diaphragm

    2._____

3. Polarizing microscopes, phase contrast microscopes, and interference microscopes differ from the standard compound light microscope in that they all use a different type of

    A. light source
    B. condenser lens
    C. objective lens
    D. eyepiece

    3._____

4. The amount of light used to view an object with a compound microscope CANNOT be varied by changing the adjustment of the

    A. Kohler illuminator
    B. iris diaphragm
    C. condenser lens
    D. binocular eyepiece

    4._____

5. When not in use, the beam and pan supports of an analytical balance should be elevated so as to

    A. prevent injury to the knife edges
    B. keep the balance level
    C. prevent dust from entering the mechanism
    D. keep the balance at a zero reading

    5._____

6. Assume that you are weighing a powder on an analytical balance with a direct-reading scale. You place a beaker on the pan and determine that the beaker weighs 13.854 grams. After adding the powder to the beaker, the readings on the balance knobs show: 100 gram - 0; 10 gram - 30; and 1 gram - 8.
The 0 mark on the Vernier scale is between 85 and 86, and the 3rd mark up on the Vernier coincides with a mark on the general scale.
The weight of the powder is _____ grams.

    A. 13.854   B. 24.999   C. 38.853   D. 52.707

    6._____

7. Which is the LEAST common blood type among the major blood groups?

    A. A   B. B   C. AB   D. 0

    7._____

8. The one of the following instruments which is NOT used to measure specific gravity of a liquid is called a

   A. hydrometer
   B. urinometer
   C. lactometer
   D. hygrometer

9. A microhemocrit test is performed and it is noted that the packed erythrocytes make up about 1/5th of the total volume of blood in the tube.
   The number of erythrocytes found in this patient is APPROXIMATELY what percentage of the number normally found?

   A. 20
   B. 50
   C. 80
   D. 100

10. The normal specific gravity of urine is APPROXIMATELY

    A. 1.000
    B. 1.020
    C. 1.050
    D. 1.100

11. When not in immediate or constant use, the electrodes of a pH meter should be

    A. stored in a refrigerator
    B. kept immersed in distilled water
    C. kept immersed in normal saline
    D. dried and the fluid emptied from inside the electrode

12. The normal pH of blood is about 7.4.
    This means that blood is

    A. strongly acidic
    B. very slightly acidic
    C. exactly neutral
    D. very slightly alkaline

13. Proper use of a clinical centrifuge includes

    A. balancing the tubes that are placed in the rotor
    B. keeping the top open when in use
    C. immediately turning to the top required speed
    D. using any available test tube for the sample

14. When using a spectrophotometer, which one of the following will result in errors in the results?

    A. Cuvet covers being used
    B. Cuvets being wiped clean of dirt and fingerprints
    C. Solutions used being turbid
    D. Color development being carried out at identical times and temperatures

15. You are required to determine the amount of glucose in a blood sample. 100 ml of a standard solution was made up containing 100 mg of glucose, and 100 ml of serum was provided. Ten ml of each was used to carry out a benedict"s test, and the results were read in a spectrophotometer. The optical density reading of the standard was 0.200, and the serum sample was 0.150.
    What was the amount of glucose in the total blood sample?
    _____ mg.

    A. 13.3
    B. 133
    C. 150
    D. 200

16. Which one of the following solutions has the LOWEST pH? 1 N _____.   16.____

    A. HCl B. acetic acid
    C. ammonium hydroxide D. NaOH

17. Which one of the following solutions has the HIGHEST pH? 1 N _____.   17.____

    A. HCl B. acetic acid
    C. ammonium hydroxide D. NaOH

18. What is the molecular weight of oxygen?   18.____

    A. 1   B. 8   C. 16   D. 40

19. A molar solution of a compound is one that contains one gram _____ of solution.   19.____

    A. molecular weight of the compound per 100 ml
    B. molecular weight of the compound per liter
    C. of the compound per 100 ml
    D. of the compound per liter

20. The SECOND reagent, and the time required for the reagent that is added to a slide when preparing a gram stain, is   20.____

    A. crystal violet (gentian violet) for 1 minute
    B. iodine for 1 minute
    C. safranin for 1 minute
    D. safranin for 20 to 30 seconds

21. The BEST staining procedure for the identification of Mycobacterium tuberculosis would be the _____ stain.   21.____

    A. gram   B. acid-fast   C. spore   D. capsule

22. Identification of filamentous fungi is *usually* based on the   22.____

    A. shape and arrangement of the spores
    B. hemolysis on blood agar plates
    C. fermentation of various sugars
    D. reaction on a TSI slant

23. Which species of bacteria would be the LEAST likely to be killed by boiling in water for 15 minutes?   23.____

    A. Staphylococcus B. Escherichia
    C. Clostridium D. Streptococcus

24. A gram stain of a streptococcus, when observed under the oil immersion lens of a microscope, will be   24.____

    A. pink-colored cocci in chains
    B. blue-colored rods
    C. blue-colored cocci in grape-like clusters
    D. blue-colored cocci in chains

25. The MOST numerous of the white blood cells is the 25.____
   A. eosinophil B. neutraphil
   C. lymphocyte D. basophil

KEY (CORRECT ANSWERS)

1.	B	11.	B
2.	A	12.	D
3.	B	13.	A
4.	D	14.	C
5.	A	15.	B
6.	B	16.	A
7.	C	17.	D
8.	D	18.	C
9.	B	19.	B
10.	B	20.	B

21. B
22. A
23. C
24. D
25. B

TEST 2

DIRECTIONS: Each question or incomplete statement is followed by several suggested answers or completions. Select the one that BEST answers the question or completes the statement. *PRINT THE LETTER OF THE CORRECT ANSWER IN THE SPACE AT THE RIGHT.*

1. Which one of the following chemicals is NOT flammable and can be used if there is a bunsen burner lit in the room?

    A. Amyl alcohol
    B. Potassium hydroxide
    C. Benzene
    D. Xylene

    1.____

2. A water or soda-type of fire extinguisher should NEVER be used to extinguish a fire in which there is

    A. alcohol
    B. paper
    C. an electrical short-circuit
    D. methanol

    2.____

3. The amount of solids in 1000 ml of urine may be estimated by multiplying the last two figures of the specific gravity by 2.6.
   If a given sample of urine has a specific gravity of 1.020, about how many grams of solid are there in 1500 ml of that urine sample?
   _____ grams.

    A. 39   B. 52   C. 78   D. 260

    3.____

4. If 17.3 grams of copper sulfate are required to make 1 liter of Benedict's solution, how much copper sulfate would be needed to make 350 ml of the solution?
   _____ grams.

    A. 1.73   B. 6.06   C. 17.3   D. 35.0

    4.____

5. 25° Centigrade MOST closely approximates which one of the following temperatures?

    A. Room temperature
    B. Body temperature
    C. Refrigerator temperature
    D. The freezing temperature of water

    5.____

6. One ml of blood is diluted in 99 ml of saline. There are 50,000 red blood cells in 1 ml of this suspension. The red cell count of the blood per ml is

    A. 503   B. 5000   C. 5×10^6 D. 50×10^3

    6.____

7. A patient who has fasted overnight is given a solution of sugar, and his blood specimens are tested at half-hour or hourly intervals to determine the amount of sugar in the blood. This test is called a

    A. GTT
    B. hematocrit
    C. CBC
    D. 2 hr P.P.

    7.____

9. A stain that would be useful in identifying starch granules in urine is

   A. gram stain
   B. iodine
   C. sudan III
   D. benzidine nitroprusside

10. A biological substance that *increases* the rate of a chemical reaction is a(n)

    A. buffer
    B. enzyme
    C. centrifuge
    D. solvent

11. A measurement of the density of a solution as compared with the density of water is called

    A. specific gravity
    B. specific conductance
    C. titration
    D. optical density

12. A substance that is added to a chemical reaction to prevent a large change in pH is a(n)

    A. enzyme   B. indicator   C. buffer   D. isotope

13. Which one of the following chemicals is NOT a pH indicator?

    A. Phenolphthalein
    B. Methyl red
    C. Methylene blue
    D. Brilliant yellow

14. The Clinitest® sugar test, used to show the amount of glucose in urine, is the *same* type of test as

    A. the Benedict's test
    B. the Biuret test
    C. Test-tape®
    D. the Kahn test

15. All of the following are lipids EXCEPT

    A. cholesterol
    B. albumin
    C. olive oil
    D. lecithin

Questions 16-20.

DIRECTIONS: Questions 16 through 20 are to be answered SOLELY on the basis of the chart shown on the next page.

3 (#2)

QUARTERLY CLINIC WORKLOAD REPORT
LABORATORIES X, Y, Z
SECOND QUARTER, 2003 AND 2004

	2004			2003		
Tests Performed	April	May	June	April	May	June
LABORATORY X Hematocrit	175	142	164	181	147	153
Urine	502	554	495	659	575	532
Sickle cells	61	85	80	54	91	74
White blood count	5	10	7	11	26	15
Hemoglobin	14	12	16	9	18	16
Pregnancy tests	203	186	214	189	207	196
Total Examinations	960	989	976	1103	1064	986
RH and STS sent to Worth St.	306	299	239	407	338	287
Tests performed by other agencies	292	313	302	356	391	333
Total Tests Sent Out	598	612	541	763	729	620
LABORATORY Y						
Hematocrit	203	157	192	147	162	198
Urine	476	516	447	386	409	422
Sickle cells	78	49	63	45	53	47
White blood count	13	7	9	16	18	13
Hemoglobin	16	19	23	14	14	9
Pregnancy tests	142	186	197	153	204	216
Total Examinations						
RH and STS sent to Worth St.	287	312	314	272	306	315
Tests performed by other agencies	323	216	254	310	381	326
Total Tests Sent Out	610	528	568	582	687	641
LABORATORY Z						
Hematocrit	203	177	184	213	201	174
Urine	452	505	478	491	349	379
Sickle cells	67	54	49	58	37	46
White blood count	11	13	14	21	10	17
Hemoglobin	19	22	24	16	17	12
Pregnancy tests	218	182	216	165	175	184
Total Examinations	970	953	965	964	789	812
RH and STS sent to Worth St.	272	298	317	314	288	303
Tests performed by other agencies	314	335	298	347	228	332
Total Tests Sent Out	586	633	615	661	516	635

16. The difference between the total examinations performed in Laboratory Y in May 2004 and May 2003 is   16._____

    A. 26   B. 68   C. 74   D. 167

17. In which of the following laboratories and years was the GREATEST number of urine tests for the months of April, May, and June performed?   17._____
    Laboratory

    A. Y in 2003   B. Y in 2004
    C. X in 2003   D. X in 2004

18. White blood count tests comprise APPROXIMATELY what percentage of the total number of examinations performed?   18._____

    A. 1%   B. 5%   C. 10%   D. 50%

19. In which one of the following laboratories and years was the total number of tests sent out in the months of April, May, and June the GREATEST?   19._____
    Laboratory

    A. X in 2003   B. Y in 2004
    C. Y in 2003   D. Z in 2004

20. In 2004, the ONLY test performed in Laboratory Z to show a steady decrease was   20._____

    A. sickle cells   B. white blood count
    C. hemoglobin   D. pregnancy tests

21. The one of the following methods of training a newly employed technician which is MOST likely to give him experience in many laboratory functions in a relatively short period of time is the _____ method.   21._____

    A. job rotation   B. sensitivity training
    C. role playing   D. conference

22. If it becomes necessary for you, as a supervisor, to give a subordinate employee confidential information, the MOST effective of the following steps to take to make sure the information is kept confidential by the employee is to   22._____

    A. tell the employee that the information is confidential and is not to be repeated
    B. threaten the employee with disciplinary action if the information is repeated
    C. offer the employee a merit increase as an incentive for keeping the information confidential
    D. remind the employee at least twice a day that the information is confidential and is not to be repeated

23. Assume that you are a supervisor of a laboratory, and one of your subordinates brings to your attention the fact that another subordinate is taking home small, inexpensive items which are city property from the laboratory.   23._____
    The BEST of the following courses of action for you to take with regard to the accused employee is to

A. make no mention of your knowledge of these thefts; the items are inexpensive anyway
B. have a discussion with the employee, since these small thefts might lead to bigger ones
C. wait until you observe the employee taking something from the laboratory and *catch him in the act*
D. give a lecture to your entire group of subordinates on honesty in the laboratory

24. Assume that you are a supervisor of a laboratory, and your supervisor informs you of a serious mistake made in the analysis of an important test performed by one of your subordinate technicians.
You should consider this action on the part of your supervisor as

    A. *undesirable;* your supervisor should have gone straight to the technician who performed the test
    B. *desirable;* it gives you an opportunity to talk to the employee, find out why the mistake was made, and try to make sure there are no more serious mistakes
    C. *undesirable;* your supervisor should have complained to the personnel office in your agency to make a note of the mistake in the technician's personnel file
    D. *desirable;* you can then discipline the employee severely to teach him to be more careful in the future

24._____

25. Assume that you, as a supervisor of a laboratory, are asked to make a recommendation to your superior on a new technician who is about to complete his probationary period. The technician's performance, even after several conferences with him, is unsatisfactory, his work habits are poor, and he does not take his work seriously.
For you to make an UNFAVORABLE recommendation about this employee, which might result in his dismissal, would be

    A. *desirable;* this action would be fair and justifiable to both the employee and the organization
    B. *undesirable;* the employee passed his Civil Service test and should eventually become satisfactory
    C. *desirable;* your superiors expect that a certain proportion of probationers will fail
    D. *undesirable;* the employee should be given a chance to work elsewhere before an evaluation of his performance is made

25._____

KEY (CORRECT ANSWERS)

1. B
2. C
3. C
4. B
5. A
6. C
7. A
8. C
9. B
10. B

11. A
12. C
13. C
14. A
15. B
16. C
17. C
18. A
19. A
20. A

21. A
22. A
23. B
24. B
25. A

GLOSSARY OF BIOLOGICAL TERMS

CONTENTS

	Page
Abdomen...... Allergen	1
Allergy ...... Antibiotics	2
Antibodies ...... Axon	3
Bacillus ...... Blood Count	4
Blood Platelets ...... Capillaries	5
Carbohydrates ...... Chlorophyll	6
Chlorophyll Bodies ...... Colon	7
Colony ...... Cro-magnon Man	8
Crop...... Diastase	9
Diatoms ...... Embryo	10
Embryology ...... Fatty Acids	11
Female Parent ...... Fruit	12
Fungus ...... Gizzard	13
Gland - Hexapods	14
Hilum ...... Inorganic	15
Insects ...... Linkage	16
Lipase .... Milt	17
Mitosis ...... Nodules	18
Notochord ...... Pepsin	19
Peripheral Nervous System .... Primates	20
Prolactin .... Retina	21
Rh Factor ..... Spawning	22
Spermatophytes .... Thallophytes	23
Thiamin .... Villus	24
White Blood Count .... Zoospore	25

GLOSSARY OF BIOLOGICAL TERMS

A

ABDOMEN - The posterior section of the body; that section behind the thorax; the stomach region in vertebrates.

ABSORPTION - The passage of dissolved substances into the villi for distribution through the body.

ACETYLCHOLINE - A neurohumor.

ACNE - An infection of the fat glands in the skin. Causes a skin eruption of the face.

ACQUIRED CHARACTERISTICS - Traits of organisms developed during their lifetime because of environmental influences.

ADAPTATION - The character of any organism or its parts which especially suits it to live in its particular environment. If an organism is not adapted to its environment, it dies.

ADDICT - A person who cannot get along without a constant supply of narcotics

ADENOIDS - Large masses of tissue in the back of the throat. May interfere with breathing, especially in children.

ADRENAL GLANDS - Two spongy masses, one above each kidney. Manufacture the hormone, adrenin, useful in emergencies.

ADRENALIN - One of the hormones secreted by the adrenals; also a neurohumor.

AGAR - A clear, jelly-like substance; used to make cultures of bacteria.

AGE OF REPTILES - The fourth geologic era, when giant reptiles dominated the earth.

AGGULTININ - Any organic substance which causes red blood cells or bacteria to clump together.

AIR SACS - The microscopic ends of the air tubes in the lungs. Oxygen and carbon dioxide are exchanged in the air sacs.

ALBINO - A plant or animal which lacks the genes for the development of color. It is usually white.

ALCOHOL - The liquid obtained by the fermentation of sugar by yeasts. Intoxicating in drinks. Used by industry and to preserve specimens.

ALGAE - Simple, green plants with roots, stems or leaves. May be one-celled or many-celled.

ALIMENTARY CANAL - The food canal. Includes the gullet, stomach, small and large intestines.

ALLERGEN - A foreign substance which causes an allergic reaction in a person sensitive to it, such as ragweed pollen.

ALLERGY - A condition in which a person is very sensitive to certain pollens, foods, dust, feathers, or other substances.

ALPINES - A race of Caucasoid stock, supposed to have inhabited originally a strip of Europe between the northern and southern regions.

ALTERNATION OF GENERATIONS - Reproduction in which the offspring are not like their parents, but like their grandparents, as in mosses and ferns; specifically, the alternation of gametophyte and sporophyte in the life cycles of some plants.

ALTITUDE SICKNESS - Bodily changes caused by the scarcity of oxygen at higher altitudes.

AMBER - A fossilized material from trees, yellow-brown in color. Found on the shores of the Baltic Sea. May contain fossil insects.

AMEBA - One of the simplest single-celled animals.

AMEBIC DYSENTERY - Disease in human beings caused by a species of ameba in the intestine.

AMINO ACIDS - The end results of protein digestion. The "building blocks" of protoplasm.

AMPHIBIA - A group of cold-blooded vertebrates, such as frogs, toads, and salamanders. Born in water and have gills which are later replaced by lungs.

ANAPHASE - Third stage in mitosis when chromosomes are pulled to opposite sides of the cell.

ANEMIA - A physical condition caused by a lack of iron (hemoglobin) or by a lack of sufficient red blood cells.

ANESTHETIC - An agent that causes a partial or complete loss of sensation or feeling.

ANGIOSPERMS - Flowering plants, one of the two subdivisions of the spermato-phytes.

ANNELIDS - Segmented worms.

ANNUAL - A plant that lives through only one growing season.

ANNUAL RING - Growth ring in woody tissue of trees and shrubs.

ANOPHELES - Mosquito that carries malaria

ANTENNA - A projecting sense organ, such as the "feeler" of insects.

ANTERIOR - Toward the front or head end of an animal that has a right and a left side.

ANTHER - The pollen-forming structure at the top of the stamen.

ANTHRAX - A disease of cattle and sheep caused by the anthrax bacillus which lives in the blood stream.

ANTHROPOLOGY - The science of man.

ANTIBIOTICS - Organic compounds made by living things and effective in stopping the growth of certain germs; penicillin is an antibiotic.

ANTIBODIES - The chemical substances produced by the blood in response to the presence of bacteria or viruses. Important in immunity.

ANTIGEN - Any substance which, when introduced into an animal's body, stimulates the production of antibodies.

ANTISEPTIC - A chemical such as iodine, that helps destroy disease germs.

ANTITOXIN - A substance produced by animal bodies that overcomes the harmful effects of the toxins of disease germs; as diphtheria antitoxin.

ANUS - Opening at the posterior end of an animal's food tube.

AORTA - The large artery through which blood is pumped from the ventricle to the general body circulation.

AORTIC ARCHES - The ten pulsating blood vessels that join the dorsal and ventral blood vessels near the anterior end of the earthworm; sometimes called "hearts" of the earthworm.

APPENDIX - Blind tube attached to the end of the caecum of the large intestine in some mammals, including man.

ARACHNIDS - The class of arthropods to which spiders, mites, and ticks belong.

ARALEN - New antimalarial drug.

ARCHEOPTERYX - Oldest known bird fossil, having some reptilian characters.

ARTERIOLES - The very smallest branches of the arteries; they lead into the capillaries.

ARTERIES - Strong, elastic blood vessels that carry blood away from the heart.

ARTHROPODS - Phylum of segmented animals with many jointed legs and an exo-skeleton; includes several classes.

ASCORBIC ACID - Vitamin C; prevents and cures scurvy.

ASEXUAL REPRODUCTION - Reproduction without sex; reproduction without the uniting of two cells; reproduction by only one parent.

ATABRINE - A synthetic drug used as a substitute for quinine in treating malaria.

ATOM - A minute particle of matter.

AURICLES - The two thin-walled upper chambers of the heart. Receive blood from large veins.

AUTONOMIC - Pertaining to that part of the nervous system which is nearly, but not quite, independent of the central nervous system.

AUXINS - Plant hormones.

AXON - The branch of a neuron which carries impulses away from the cell body.

B

BACILLUS - A rod-shaped bacterium.

BACTERIA - Single-celled, microscopic plants, lacking in chlorophyll. Causes decay, disease and fermentation.

BALANCE OF NATURE - The condition in nature in which the plant and animal populations are in normal balance with each other, so that no one species becomes overabundant; well illustrated in a balanced aquarium; also called NATURAL EQUILIBRIUM.

BANDING - The process of attaching a numbered metal band or tag to an animal in order to find out where it travels.

BEHAVIOR - The responses of an organism to stimuli.

BENIGN - A new growth of cells of comparatively harmless nature, such as warts

BERIBERI - A disease resulting from a lack of vitamin Bi (thiamin). Causes paralysis of the nervous system and loss of appetite.

BICUSPIDS - Two-pointed teeth of mammals, immediately in front of the molars.

BIENNIAL - A plant that lives through two growing seasons, and bears flowers and fruits only in the second season.

BILE - A greenish-yellow, bitter liquid made by the liver and poured in the small intestine. Changes oils and fats into a milky fluid.

BINOMIAL SYSTEM - The system of naming plant and animal species; the two-name system.

BIOLOGICAL CONTROL - Control which uses natural enemies of insects or other pests in the fight against them.

BIOME - Any community of plants and animals.

BIOPSY - The removal and examination of a bit of tissue from a living body.

BIRDS - Class of vertebrates that have feathers and breathe by lungs throughout life.

BLADDER - The organ which receives urine from the kidneys and stores it for a time.

BLASTODERM - The first layer of cells formed by the early divisions of the ovum of the chick and many other animals.

BLASTULA - The hollow ball of cells constituting an early stage of the embryonic development of many animals.

BLOOD - A liquid tissue consisting of water, minerals, and red and white blood cells. An adult has about six quarts of blood.

BLOOD COUNT - A count of the number of red or white blood cells in a cubic millimeter of blood.

BLOOD PLATELETS - Small bodies in the blood which, under suitable conditions, break down, releasing a clot-starting substance.

BOLL WEEVIL - A beetle whose grub destroys the cotton plant.

BRAIN - A large mass of nerve cells and their fibers that fills the skull. Consists of the cerebrum, cerebellum and medulla.

BREATHING - The taking in of oxygen and giving off of carbon dioxide by living things. Some biologists limit the term of this process in animals.

BRONCHIAL TUBES - Tubes branching from the lower end of the windpipe and leading into the lung tissue.

BRONZE - A hard metal made of copper and tin. Used by men in the Bronze Age before iron was discovered.

BRYOPHYTES - The phylum which includes the mosses and liverworts.

BUDDING - A form of asexual reproduction in which a small bud of the parent produces a new individual, as in some yeasts, sponges, and hydras; also the grafting of a bud from one tree to another, as in peaches.

BULB - An underground part of a plant, such as the onion. Rich in food value and capable of producing a new plant the next season.

C

CAECUM - A pouch or tube closed at one end, as the end of the large intestine in man, to which the appendix is attached; pyloric caeca of fishes open into the intestine just below the stomach.

CALCIUM - A chemical found in many vegetables and in milk. Important in building healthy bones and teeth.

CALORIE - A unit of measure of the energy obtainable from food.

CALORIE, GREAT - The amount of heat required to raise 1,000 grams of water from $3.5°C.$ to $4.5°C.$; used in reference to foods; the calorie used in physics is the amount of heat required to raise one gram of water from $3.5°C.$ to $4.5°C.$

CAMBIUM - A layer of living cells from which new xylem and phloem cells are formed in the stems and some roots of dicots and gymnosperms.

CAMBRIAN - First period of the third geologic era.

CANDLING - The examination of a hen's egg by placing it in front of a bright light in a darkened room. Used to detect undesirable eggs.

CANINES - The tearing teeth of mammals; very prominent in carnivores.

CAPILLARIES - The smallest blood vessels, with walls one-cell thick. Connect arteries to veins.

CARBOHYDRATES - A class of foods (starches and sugars) composed of carbon, hydrogen, and oxygen. The number of hydrogen atoms in a molecule and graphite; a component part of protoplasm.

CARBON DIOXIDE - A compound of carbon and oxygen, each molecule of which contains one atom of carbon and two atoms of oxygen.

CARNIVORES - Order of the flesh-eating mammals, such as lions, tigers, cats, and dogs.

CARTILAGE - A smooth, shiny type of connective tissue on the ends of bones. Also called gristle.

CATTALO - The offspring obtained by crossing a cow with a bison (buffalo).

CAUCASOIDS - One of the three main stems or stocks of living man.

CAUDAL - Pertaining to the tail.

CELL - A unified mass of protoplasm, usually composed of a nucleus and cytoplasm surrounded by a cell membrane and by a cell wall in plants; the unit of structure of living things.

CELL DIFFERENTIATION - The changing of embryonic cells into specialized cells, as muscle, wood, nerve.

CELL MEMBRANE - Thin bounding layer that covers animal and young plant cells; also the thin layer of cytoplasm that lines the cell wall of mature plant cells; also called the CYTOPLASMIC MEMBRANE.

CELL THEORY - The theory that all living things are made of cells and cell products; first advanced by Schleiden and Schwann in 1838-1839.

CELLULOSE - Organic compound found in the cell wall of nearly all plant cells, but not commonly found in animal cells.

CELL WALL - The hard, woody coating around plant cells. Helps to protect and support the cell. Dried lumber consists of cell walls.

CENTRAL CYLINDER - Woody tissue in the center of roots.

CENTRAL NERVOUS SYSTEM - The brain and spinal cord of a vertebrate.

CEREBELLUM - The part of the brain lying behind and below the cerebrum. Controls muscular coordination.

CEREBRAL HEMORRHAGE - A hemorrhage in the brain, usually followed by paralysis.

CEREBRUM - The upper part of the brain, consisting of two halves, each with deep grooves. Controls thought, speech, memory, and voluntary acts.

CHEMICAL CHANGE - A change in matter that involves a change in the kinds of atoms in the molecules.

CHLOROPHYLL - The green material found in the cells of green plants. Important in making starch and sugar.

CHLOROPHYLL BODIES - Small bodies found inside the cells of green plants. Contain the green chlorophyll which helps carry on photosynthesis.

CHLORPOPLAST - Small definite body of cytoplasm containing chlorophyll, found in some cells of green plants.

CHORDATES - Phylum of animals having a dorsal supporting rod of gristle, either in the embryo, as in vertebrates, or throughout life, as in the lancelet, and having a dorsal hollow nerve cord.

CHOROID COAT - The dark coat of the vertebrate eye.

CHROMATIN - Material in the cell nucleus which takes a dye readily. Forms the chromosomes.

CHROMOSOMES - Threads of chromatin seen in dividing cells. Contain the genes.

CILIA - Hair-like threads that beat back and forth. Enable paramecia to swim. Are present on cells that line the breathing passages, and help remove dust.

CITRUS FRUITS - Acid fruits, such as oranges and lemons. Rich in vitamin C.

CLEANED-TILLED CROPS - Crops which are cultivated in rows, such as potatoes and corn.

CLIMAX - Final stage in a plant succession, tending to persist indefinitely; examples: beech-maple forest, wheat-grass grassland.

CLOSED SEASON - A time of year when the hunting of certain animals is forbidden by law.

CLOSE-GROWING CROPS - Crops like clover, hay, and wheat which grow close together and cover the soil.

CLOT - A jelly-like mass which forms when blood leaves a blood vessel. Consists of a mass of fibers and blood cells. Prevents further bleeding.

COCCI - Bacteria that are round in shape. Include bacteria that cause pneumonia and scarlet fever.

COCHLEA - The portion of the inner ear in which sound vibrations reach the endings of the auditory nerve.

CODLING MOTH - Chief insect enemy of apples; the larva is the so-called apple worm.

COELENTERATES - The phylum which includes the corals, hydras, jellyfish, and sea anemones.

COLCHICINE - A chemical which is applied to plants in order to double the number of chromsomes. May result in new varieties.

COLD-BLOODED - Pertaining to a vertebrate whose temperature changes with that of its surroundings.

COLLAR CELLS - Flagellated cells in the lining of the cavities in sponges, whose flagella keep a current of water flowing through the body.

COLON - The large intestine.

COLONY - Group of individuals organically joined together, with each individual more or less independent, as in some of the protozoa.

COMMON ANCESTOR - An organism that was an ancester of two or more species or varieties of organisms.

COMPOSITES - A family of flowering plants having a compound head of flowers, such as dandelions or daisies.

COMPOST - Mixed fertilizing materials, such as heaps of decaying crop residue,

COMPOUND - A substance whose molecule is composed of two or more kinds of atoms in chemical combination.

CONDITIONED REFLEX OR REACTION - Behavior in response to a stimulus other than the usual or normal one; an acquired response.

CONE - Seed-bearing organ of evergreens and other naked-seeded plants.

CONJUGATION - The uniting of two cells, often of similar size and appearance, as in spirogyra and paramecium.

CONTACT SPRAYS - Sprays that kill insects upon touching them.

CONTOUR PLOWING - A method of plowing a hillside so that the furrows go around the hill instead of up and down.

CONTROL - A part of an experiment which tests or checks the result. Provides a basis for comparison.

CORNEA - Transparent layer covering the front of the vertebrate eye.

CORONARY ARTERIES - The arteries which supply the tissues of the heart.

CORONARY HEART DISEASE - Heart condition in which coronary arteries decrease in diameter.

CORONARY THROMBOSIS - The formation of a blood clot in a coronary artery.

CORPUSCLE - Blood cell; a red blood corpuscle is a blood cell that carries oxygen; a white blood corpuscle is a blood cell that aids in the defense against germ attack.

CORTEX - The tissue in a root or stem that lies between the fibrovascular tissue and the epidermis; the outer layers of an organ such as the brain.

COTYLEDON - Seed leaf; single in mbnocots, double in dicots; numerous in naked-seeded spermatophytes.

CRANIAL NERVES - Nerves from the brain; 12 pairs in man.

CRETIN - One born with an abnormally deficient thyroid or none at all. Usually idiocy results unless thyroxin is given regularly in childhood.

CRO-MAGNON MAN - A type of prehistoric man very much like men of today. Lived in caves and decorated them with animal paintings.

CROP - An enlarged portion of the food tube of earthworms and birds in which food is stored when first swallowed; also plants for harvest, as a crop of corn.

CROP RESIDUES — Remains of crops, after harvesting, such as straw and stubble.

CROP ROTATION - A plan which prevents the loss of important soil minerals over a period of time. Different crops are planted in an area each year.

CROSSBREEDING - A breeding process for combining the traits of plants or animals of two different kinds.

CROSSING OVER - The breaking of two adjacent chromosomes, during separation, with the subsequent union of a fragment (or fragments) of one with a fragment (or fragments) of the other.

CRUSTACEA - Class of arthropods to which the crayfish and barnacle belong.

CULTURE - The growth of bacteria or other organisms in suitable surroundings, as a culture of staphylococci on agar. A pure culture is a culture containing only one kind of organism, as a pure culture of diphtheria bacilli;. a culture medium is a particular material, such as agar or beef broth, in or on which bacteria are grown; also man's learned way of life.

CUTTING - A piece of a root, stem or leaf which can be planted to produce a complete new plant.

CYCAD - A seed plant of the naked-seeded class.

CYST - A sac, or an encased resting stage such as that of the trichina.

CYTOLOGY - The study of cells.

CYTOPLASM - That part of the cell that lies outside the nucleus. Carries on all life activities except reproduction.

D

DAPHNIA - A tiny water flea found in ponds. Invertebrate, related to the lobster.

DEFICIENCY DISEASE - Disease caused by lack of vitamins, minerals, amino acids or other necessary elements in the diet.

DENDRITES - The branches of a neuron which carry impulses toward the cell body.

DEOXYGENATED BLOOD - Blood that has lost its oxygen to the cells.

DEPRESSANT - A drug or other agent that slows down such vital body functions as breathing rate and heartbeat.

DIABETES - A disease in which sugar is incompletely burned in the body. Caused by failure of the pancreas island cells to make the hormone, insulin.

DIAPHRAGM - The large muscle which separates the chest cavity from the abdomen. Makes breathing possible by contracting and relaxing.

DIASTASE - The enzyme which digests starch in a sprouting grain of corn.

DIATOMS - One-celled algae that have glassy shells.

DICOTYLEDONS - Subclass of flowering plants having two cotyledons in the seed, netted-veined leaves, and one or more rings of wood in the stem; they include most of our common flowering plants, such as beans, geraniums, hardwood trees; commonly called dicots.

DIFFUSION - Spreading of molecules from areas of their greatest density toward areas of less density; sometimes applied loosely to any intermingling of molecules.

DIGESTION - A process of chemical change that prepares food for absorption. Goes on in the mouth, stomach, and small intestine with the aid of enzymes.

DINOSAURS - Extinct reptiles, many of enormous size. Died out sixty million years ago.

DIPLOID NUMBER - Twice the number of chromosomes found in a gamete; 48 is the diploid number in man.

DOMINANT - The trait in a contrasting pair (such as tallness and dwarfness) that shows in a hybrid; tallness is dominant in peas.

DORSAL - Pertaining to the back or upper side of an animal.

DUCKBILL - A rare Australian mammal that lays eggs.

DUCTLESS GLAND - A gland that secretes a hormone directly into the blood stream and does not deliver its secretion through a duct.

DUODENUM - The first part of the small intestine leading from the stomach.

E

ECHINODERMS - The phylum of the spiny-skinned animals, such as the starfish, sea urchins, and their relatives.

ECOLOGY - Biology that deals with the relations of organisms to each other and to their nonliving environment.

ECTODERM - The outer layer of cells of a gastrula, an embryological term; has also been applied to the outer body layer of cells in hydra and other adult coelenterates.

EGG - The sex cell produced in the ovary of the female. Develops into an embryo if fertilized by a sperm cell.

ELECTRON - One of the constituents of all atoms; a single charge of negative electricity.

ELEMENT - A substance whose molecules contain only one kind of atom; 96 elements are known.

ELODEA - A water plant belonging to the dicots.

EMBOLISM - A blood clot that has been carried away from its original site and lodged in a blood vessel too small to let it pass.

EMBRYO - The form of a plant or animal in the beginning stage of life.

EMBRYOLOGY - The study of the growth and development of embryos.

ENDODERM - The inside layer of cells of a gastrula, an embryological term; has also been applied to the inner layer of hydra and other adult coelenterates.

END ORGANS - Sensitive outer endings of sensory neurons; better called receptors.

ENDOSPERM - The storage tissue in monocot seeds and in a few dicot seeds, such as the castor bean.

ENERGY - The capacity to do work.

ENTOMOLOGY - Study of insects.

ENZYMES - Substances made in gland cells, that can cause chemical changes. Example: pepsin, which digests proteins.

EPIDERMIS - The outer layer of cells on an organ or organism; skin.

EPIGLOTTIS - The flap of tissue that covers the top of the windpipe during swallowing.

EPITHELIAL TISSUE - Covering tissue, including epithelium (skin) and endo-thelium (lining tissue).

EPOCH - A subdivision of a geological period.

ERA - One of the five main divisions of geologic time.

EROSION - The wearing away of the earth's surface by water, ice, and winds.

ESOPHAGUS - That portion of the food tube which connects mouth region or pharynx and crop or stomach.

EUGENICS - That branch of genetics which aims at improving mankind by breeding; the science of being well born.

EUGLENA - A one-celled plant-animal.

EUSTACHIAN TUBE - Tube connecting the middle ear with the throat.

EVOLUTION - The process of change by which plants and animals develop from simpler to more complex forms.

EXOSKELETON - External skeleton.

EYESPOT - Spot of pigment, usually red, sensitive to light.

F

F_1 GENERATION - First generation of offspring from a cross.

F_2 GENERATION - Offspring of the F_1 generation.

FATTY ACIDS - The end-products of fat digestion. Can pass into the villi.

FEMALE PARENT - The parent that produces the ovum or egg.

FERMENTATION - A chemical change brought about by enzymes produced by microbes. In the making of beer or wine, yeasts ferment sugars into alcohol and carbon dioxide.

FERTILIZATION - The uniting of a sperm nucleus with an egg nucleus. Results in the development of an embryo.

FERTILIZED EGG - The cell formed by the union of the egg and the sperm; an egg after a sperm has united with it; also called a zygote.

FERTILIZER - Chemical substance added to the soil to feed plants. Also used to replace the minerals removed by former crops.

FIBRINOGEN - A chemical in the blood which helps the blood to clot. Forms fibers that entangle blood cells.

FIBROVASCULAR BUNDLE - A group of xylem and phloem cells, as the stringy fibers in celery.

FILAMENT - Thread-shaped alga or fungus composed of cells end to end; the stalk of a stamen; the projections on a fish's gill that are filled with blood.

FISHES - Vertebrates that breathe by gills throughout life, and usually possess scales and fins.

FLAGELLATE - A one-celled animal bearing one or more flagella.

FLAGELLUM - A long hairlike or whiplike projection from a cell.

FLATWORMS - Phylum which includes the tapeworms, planaria, and their relatives .

FLUORINE - A chemical used to help prevent tooth decay. Small amounts may be placed in a city's water supply.

FLYWAYS - The pathways in the sky which are used by migrating birds each season.

FOCAL INFECTION - A localized pocket of infection, as at the rooth of a tooth or in a tonsil; always a threat to the health.

FOLIC ACID - A B vitamin which prevents severe anemias.

FOOD CHAIN - A series of organisms, each of which depends for its food on the one following it in the series.

FORTIFIED - Given added value (in nutrition). A food is fortified when an important food substance is added to it. Margarine is fortified with Vitamin A. Milk may be fortified with Vitamin D.

FOSSIL - The remains of ancient plants and animals sometimes found in rock layers.

FRATERNAL TWINS - Twins developed from two separate fertilized ova.

FRUCTOSE - Fruit sugar; a simple sugar, $C_6H_{12}O_6$.

FRUIT - A ripened ovary, together with any intimately connected parts.

FUNGUS (plural - fungi) - Simple plant, of the thallophyte phylum, lacking chlorophyll. Includes bacteria, yeasts, molds, mushrooms, rusts, and smuts. Lives on dead or living plants and animals.

G

GALL BLADDER - A round sac on the liver which stores bile and releases it into the small intestine.

GAMETES - Reproductive cells which fuse; the female gamete is called an ovum or egg, and the male gamete a sperm.

GAMETOPHYTE - In an alternation of generations, the plant that produces the gametes.

GANGLION - A group or mass of cell bodies of neurons.

GASTRIC JUICE - The digestive juice made by the stomach. Digests protein. Made of water, weak-acid, and pepsin.

GASTRULA - The two-layered folded-in stage or jellyfishlike stage of many animal embryos; it consists of ectoderm and endoderm.

GEIGER COUNTER - An instrument that ticks when near any radioactive substance.

GEL - A substance consisting of a network of fibers in which are suspended particles of a liquid; cooked egg white is a gel.

GENES - The invisible particles in the cell nucleus which control the inheritance of traits.

GENUS - The group (between family and species) named first in the scientific name of a plant or animal; a genus is a group of related species.

GERM - Any one-celled plant or animal which causes disease.

GERMINATION - The sprouting of a spore or seed.

GESTATION PERIOD - Time required for a mammal embryo to develop from fertilization to birth.

GILL - An animal organ in which the blood absorbs oxygen out of the air that is dissolved in water.

GILL ARCH - The bony arch supporting a fish's gill.

GILL FILAMENTS - The fingerlike projections of a fish's gill; these filaments are filled with blood.

GILL RAKERS - The projections from the side of the gill arch; these fit together and form a strainer in the back of the fish's mouth.

GILL SLIT - The opening on the side of a fish's throat where the water current used in breathing leaves the mouth and flows out over the gill filaments

GIZZARD - The muscular stomach of earthworms and birds and other animals, in which the food is crushed and partly digested.

GLAND - An organized group of cells which make and pour out juices such as enzymes and hormones.

GLOTTIS - The opening from the mouth into the windpipe in air-breathing vertebrates.

GLUCOSE - A simple sugar that can pass through cell membranes. Turns Benedict's solution brick red.

GLYCERINE - A clear liquid obtained after the digestion of fats.

GLYCOGEN - A carbohydrate stored in the liver and present in muscles; often called animal starch.

GOITER - A swelling of the thyroid gland in the neck. Often caused by a lack of iodine in the diet.

GONORRHEA - An infection of the reproductive system, caused by bacteria.

GRAFTING - The act of inserting a bud or a twig into a slit in the bark of a rooted tree. When the tissues join, the new bud or twig is nourished by the tree.

GRANTIA - A genus of sponges.

GREEN-MANURE CROPS - Crops that are planted to be plowed under, as rye and many legumes often are.

GROWTH HORMONE - Hormone produced by the pituitary gland. Promotes normal growth. Too much in childhood may result in giantism.

GUARD CELLS - The two cells on either side of a leaf's stomate which regulati the size of the opening.

GULLET - The food tube which connects the mouth to the stomach.

GYMNOSPERMS - Plants of the spermatophyte phylum that have naked seeds, as pines, cycads, and their allies.

H

HAPLOID NUMBER - The number of chromosomes in a gamete; 24 is the haploid number in man.

HEMOGLOBIN - An iron-rich chemical found in the red blood cells. Combines with oxygen in the lungs and gives it up to tissue cells.

HEMOPHILIA - A serious physical condition in which blood fails to clot properly. Inherited by sons from mothers who are carriers.

HERB - Any seed plant that does not develop annual rings of persistent woody tissue.

HERMAPHRODITE - An animal having both male and female reproductive organs, as an earthworm.

HEXAPODS - The class of true insects in the arthropod phylum, also called the INSECTA.

HILUM - The scar showing where a seed was attached in a pod, as on a lima bean.

HORMONE - A chemical made by certain glands and poured into the blood stream Includes insulin, adrenin, thyroxin and growth hormones.

HOST - An organism within or upon which a parasite lives.

HUMORS-AQUEOUS AND VITREOUS - The liquids that fill the two chambers in the vertebrate eye.

HUMUS - Organic matter in the soil.

HYBRID - A plant or animal which has two different genes for a trait, as the offspring of pure tall and dwarf peas. Also, the offspring of two different kinds of plants or animals.

HYBRID VIGOR - Increased size or strength of a hybrid, as in the cattalo.

HYDRA - Fresh-water relative of the jellyfish.

HYDROPHYTES - Plants that grow in wet places, such as water lillies.

HYPOCOTYL - Root region of an embryo plant within the seed.

I

ICHNEUMONS - A family of insects useful to man because they parasitize many harmful insects.

IDIOT - A person with the mental ability of a three-year-old child. I.Q. between 0 and 25.

IMBECILE - A person who is mentally deficient. I.Q. between 25 and 50.

INBORN REFLEX - A pathway in the nervous system of an animal that functions without training or practice.

INCISORS - The cutting teeth on the front of mammal jaws.

INCOMPLETE DOMINANCE - A situation in which neither gene of a pair is dominant. Result is a blending of traits. A red snapdragon crossed with a white results in a pink flower.

INCOMPLETE RESPIRATION - Type of respiration in which oxidation of food is not completed, but stops when alcohol and carbon dioxide (or other substances) are produced; fermentation is an example of incomplete respiration carried on by yeasts and some bacteria.

INCUBATION - The period of time it takes to hatch a bird out of the egg. Also the time it takes for a disease to appear after the first contact with the germ.

INFRARED - Those lights rays just beyond the red end of the visible spectrum.

INOCULATION - The introduction of bacteria or a virus into surroundings suited to their growth, as the inoculation of clover seeds with nitrogen-fixing bacteria or the inoculation of persons with cowpox virus to produce immunity against smallpox.

INORGANIC - Term applied to anything that is not alive and not produced by living things.

INSECTS - Class of arthropods that have three body regions and six legs, and usually wings.

INSULIN - The hormone made by the pancreas island cells. Helps the body burn and store sugar, and prevents diabetes.

INVERTEBRATES - Animals which do not have a backbone. Includes worms, jelly-fishes, clams, insects, lobsters.

INVOLUNTARY MUSCLE - A group of cells which contract when stimulated by nerve fibers. Not controlled by the mind.

IODINE - A chemical used by the thyroid gland in making thyroxin. Prevents some types of goiter.

ION - An electrified particle of matter formed when a neutral atom or other particle loses or gains one or more electrons.

IRIS - The colored tissue surrounding the pupil of the eye. Controls the amount of light entering the eye.

IRRITABILITY - The capacity of protoplasm to receive impulses from and to respond to stimuli.

IRON - A chemical which is needed in making hemoglobin. Prevents anemia.

ISLETS - Clusters of insulin-producing cells in the pancreas.

ISONIAZID - A recently-discovered drug which may prove useful in fighting tuberculosis.

ISOTOPE - Any of two or more forms of the same element which differ only in the number of neutrons their atoms contain; a radioisotope is a radio-active isotope.

L

LACTEAL - End of a lymph vessel in the center of a villus; it absorbs digested fats out of the intestine.

LARVA - The wormlike stage of an insect having complete metamorphosis, as a caterpillar; the young form of various animals where markedly different from the adult.

LEGUME - Any plant that has a blossom shaped like a pea and a pod of the pea or bean type; also used to refer to the podlike fruit of such plants.

LENS - The focusing portion of the eye.

LENTICEL - Breathing pore in the young bark of trees.

LICHENS - Compound plants consisting of algae and fungi which live intimately together; common on barren rock surfaces.

LIMESTONE - A type of sedimentary rock that is rich in lime.

LINKAGE - A term used to refer to the fact that the genes in a given chromosome are linked together and hence transmitted together to the offspring.

LIPASE - An enzyme in the pancreatic and intestinal juices which aids in digesting fats, but only when bile is present.

LIVER - The largest gland in the body. Makes and pours out bile and stores extra sugar as animal starch.

LIVERWORTS - Relatives of mosses, belong to the same phylum.

LYMPH - That part of the blood serum which is outside the blood vessels; it surrounds each living cell; it circulates slowly back toward the heart through lymph vessels and re-enters the blood stream near the heart.

LYMPH NODE - One of the masses of tissue through which the lymph passes on its way back toward the heart; a lymph gland.

M

MAGGOT - Larval stage of a fly.

MALE PARENT - The parent that produces the male gametes or sperms.

MALTOSE - A sugar formed from starch by the action of ptyalin; $C_{12}H_{22}O_{11}$.

MARSUPIALS - Pouched mammals.

MEDULLA - The bulb-like part at the bottom of the brain. Connects the brain to the spinal cord. Controls breathing and circulation.

MESODERM - The middle layer of cells of an embryonic stage developed from the gastrula or from a similar stage.

MESOPHYTES - Plants that grow in soil with medium amounts of water.

METABOLISM - The sum total of the chemical changes going on in a living organism; BASAL

METABOLISM TEST - measures the rate at which oxygen is used in the human body; useful in diagnosis of thyroid diseases.

METAMORPHOSIS - Marked and more or less sudden changes in the development of young animals, as the change of an insect larva into a pupa or pupa into an adult or a tadpole into a frog; in insects INCOMPLETE METAMORPHOSIS is that in which the young resemble the adult in general form; COMPLETE METAMORPHOSIS is that in which the young do not resemble the adult.

METAPHASE - Second stage in mitosis during which the double chromosomes grouj along a middle plane.

MICRON - 1/1000 of a millimeter or 1/25,000 of an inch; the unit used in measuring microscopic objects.

MICROPYLE - The little opening near the hilum of a seed; the pollen tube usually enters the ovule through it.

MILT - The material produced by the testes of male fish. Contains the sperm cells.

MITOSIS - Cell division in which the chromosomes duplicate themselves.

MOLLUSK - A soft-bodied invertebrate. Usually has a shell outside the body. Includes the snail, the octopus, and the clam.

MORON - A person with an I.Q. between 50 and 70.

MORPHOLOGY - Study of the form and structure of plants and animals.

MULE - The hybrid resulting from crossing a male donkey with a female horse.

MUTATION - A sudden change in a gene. The new trait which results is inheritable.

MUTATION THEORY - De Vries's theory of evolution.

MYCELIUM - Fine white threads that make up the main plant body of many fungi, such as molds and mushrooms.

MYRIAPODS - A class of arthropods, including the centipedes and millipedes.

MYXEDEMA - A disease caused by lack of thyroxin, characterized by puffy fatness.

N

NATURAL SELECTION - A theory which states that nature weeds out the unfit, allowing only the superior to reproduce, and pass on their good traits. In time better types of plants and animals develop.

NEUROHUMORS - Substances produced by neurons, such as acetylcholine or adrenalin.

NEURON - A nerve cell; ASSOCIATIVE - a central transferring neuron in a reflex arc; SENSORY - a neuron along which impulses travel in toward the central nervous system; MOTOR - a neuron along which impulses travel outward from the central nervous system.

NEUTRON - One of the constituents of the nucleus of nearly all atoms; an uncharged particle in the nucleus.

NIACIN - The recently accepted name of the antipellagra vitamin, formerly called nicotinic acid.

NITRATE - A compound in which nitrogen is combined with oxygen and at least one other element, such as potassium; example, KNO_3.

NITROGEN - An element which makes up 80 per cent of the air. Important in protein manufacture in plants.

NITROGEN CYCLE - The course of the element nitrogen from the air into organic compounds in living things and back into the air again.

NITROGEN-FIXING BACTERIA - Bacteria usually found in the roots of peas, clover, and alfalfa. Take in nitrogen and change it to a form useful to green plants.

NODULES - Little lumps on the roots of clover and other legumes, in which nitrogen-fixing bacteria live.

NOTOCHORD - A lengthwise elastic rod of cartilage lying just below the nerve cord in all chordates, at least in the embryo.

NUCLEOPROTEIN - Any protein composed of a protein plus a nucleic acid molecule; germs and viruses are believed to be nucleoproteins.

NUCLEUS - A thick, round structure in the cell, containing the chromatin. Takes part in the reproduction of the cell and controls heredity.

NYMPH - The young of certain insects, such as grasshoppers and termites, that have incomplete metamorphosis.

O

ORGAN - A group of tissues organized to do one job. Example: the heart, stomach, skin, eyes, or kidney.

ORGANIC COMPOUND - Any compound that contains carbon is usually called an organic compound, although there are exceptions, such as carbon dioxide.

OSMOSIS - A special kind of diffusion, in which water molecules diffuse through a semipermeable membrane.

OVIDUCT - The duct from the ovary through which eggs are passed; in some animals the fertilized eggs develop in the oviduct.

OVULE - The part containing the egg nucleus in flowering plants. After fertilization, each ovule develops into a seed.

OVUM - An egg cell.

P

PALISADE LAYER - A layer of green cells just under the upper epidermis of a leaf.

PANCREAS - A gland below the stomach. Makes digestive enzymes which are poured into the small intestines, and contains island cells which make insulin .

PARAMECIUM - A common protozoan found in ponds. Moves by means of cilia on its surface.

PARASITE - An animal or plant that obtains its food by living inside or on another living thing. Includes the tapeworm, hookworm, louse, ringworm, and many bacteria.

PARATHYROIDS - Glands located near the thyroid; the parathyroids secrete a hormone which regulates the body's assimilation of calcium.

PASTEURIZATION - A process in which a substance (such as milk) is heated to 150°F. and quickly chilled in order to kill disease germs.

PELLAGRA - A severe skin rash and nerve illness caused by a lack of niacin (a B vitamin).

PEPSIN - The enzyme produced by the gastric glands that line the walls of the stomach. Starts the digestion of protein.

PERIPHERAL NERVOUS SYSTEM - All parts of the nervous system except the brain and spinal cord.

PERISTALSIS - The progressive contraction of circular muscles in the food tube of higher animals which forces the food onward.

PETALS - The colored parts of a flower which help to attract insects.

PHARYNX - The anterior end of the food tube of many animals.

PHLOEM - Food-conducting cells in the roots, stems, and leaves of ferns and seed plants.

PHOTOSYNTHESIS - The process by which a green plant combines water and carbon dioxide to make sugar or starch. Sunlight is necessary to do this. Oxygen is the by-product.

PHYLUM - One of the main groups of the plant or animal kingdom.

PINEAL GLAND - Ductless gland situated at the base of the brain.

PISTIL - The female part of the flower which contains the ovary. Grows into a fruit after fertilization.

PISTILLATE FLOWERS - Flowers that contain pistils but no stamens.

PITUITARY GLAND - A gland the size of a pea, lying in the skull just below the brain. Controls growth and other life activities, and makes a number of hormones. The "master gland."

PLACENTA - A membrane attached to the wall of the uterus. Food passes from the blood of the mother to the embryo by way of the placenta.

PLANARIA - A common flatworm.

PLASMA - The liquid part of the blood. Contains antibodies, hormones, and digested foods.

PLATELETS - Tiny particles in the blood which help the blood to clot.

PLEUROCOCCUS - A single-celled green plant, common in the green smears on the shady side of tree trunks.

PLUMULE - That portion of a seed-plant embryo which grows into the shoot.

POLLEN - The powder-like particles made in the stamens of plants. Each pollen grain develops a sperm nucleus when it sprouts on the tip of the pistil.

POLLEN TUBE - The part of a sprouting pollen grain sent down the pistil. The sperm nucleus inside this tube is delivered to the egg nucleus in the ovule.

POLLINATION - The transfer of pollen from a stamen to a pistil either by insects or by wind.

PORIFERA - The phylum of the sponges.

PRIMATES - Order of mammals that walk more or less upright, including monkeys, apes, and man.

PROLACTIN - A hormone secreted by the pituitary body; stimulates mothering behavior and the secretion of milk in mammals.

PROPHASE - First stage of mitosis during which each chromosome duplicates itself, gene by gene, and the chromosomes shorten by contracting into tight spirals.

PROTEIN - A basic food substance containing carbon, hydrogen, oxygen, and nitrogen. Necessary for growth and repair of tissues. Found in meat, milk, beans, and many other foods.

PROTHALLIUM - The gametophyte of the ferns and their relatives.

PROTHROMBIN - The substance in blood plasma from which thrombin is made; necessary if blood is to clot.

PROTON - One of the constituents of the nucleus of all atoms; a single charge of positive electricity.

PROTOPLASM - The living material found in the cells of all living things. Carries on all the life activities.

PROTOZOA - One-celled animals, such as the ameba and paramecium.

PSEUDOPODIUM - Projected lobe of cytoplasm by which an ameba moves.

PTERIDOPHYTES - Phylum of the ferns, club mosses, and horsetails.

PTOSIS - The falling down of an organ or part of the body, as the stomach or an eyelid.

PTYALIN - A digestive enzyme in saliva which aids in changing starch to maltose.

PUPA - The more or less quiescent stage between larva and adult in the complete metamorphosis of insects.

PURE - A term used in genetics to refer to a plant or animal carrying both genes alike in a given pair; as a pure tall or a pure dwarf pea; pure tails produce only tall descendants when self-pollinated.

R

RECEPTORS - The endings of nerves. Sensitive to touch, chemicals, taste, sound, temperature, and other stimuli.

RECESSIVE TRAIT - A trait that does not show up in a hybrid. Hidden by the dominant trait.

REDUCTION DIVISION - Cell division in which the number of chromosomes is reduced to half; it usually occurs in animals when sperms and eggs are being formed.

RENNIN - An anzyme in the gastric juice which curds milk.

RESPIRATION - The oxidation of food within a living cell; external evidences may be the entrance of oxygen and release of carbon dioxide; sometimes used to include breathing in higher animals.

RETINA - A layer of light-sensitive cells in the vertebrate eye.

RH FACTOR - A bloodtype found in most people which sometimes causes damage to the blood of babies.

RIBOFLAVIN - Vitamin 62. Found in milk, lean meat, eggs, and many vegetables Necessary for normal growth.

RICKETTSIA - A type of minute disease-producing agents that may be intermediate between bacteria and viruses, causing typhus fever and a few other diseases.

ROTIFER - A small many-celled animal often found among protozoa.

S

SANDSTONE - A type of sedimentary rock formed from sand under great pressure.

SCHICK TEST - A test to determine if a person is immune to diphtheria. A small quantity of diphtheria toxin is placed under the skin. If a red spot appears, the person lacks immunity.

SCION - The bud or twig that is attached to the stock in grafting.

SCURVY - A condition caused by lack of vitamin C. The teeth loosen, joints ache, and blood vessels break under the skin.

SEDIMENTARY ROCK - Rock made from sediment that has been under pressure; rock characterized by layers; stratified rock.

SEED - A developed ovule consisting of a protective coat, stored food, and an embryo plant.

SEED DISPERSAL - The scattering of seeds to places more or less distant from the parent plant.

SEED FERNS - Extinct plants of fern type, but bearing seeds instead of spores

SEED LEAVES - The two halves of a seed (as in the bean) containing stored food. Help feed the sprouting baby plant.

SEMICIRCULAR CANALS - The portion of the inner ear in which the sense of balance is located.

SEMIPERMEABLE MEMBRANE - A membrane through which some kinds of molecules diffuse readily while others diffuse with difficulty or not at all.

SEPALS - The tiny, green, leaf-like parts found below the petals. Protect the closed flower buds.

SETA - One of the bristles used by an earthworm in locomotion.

SEX-LINKED GENES - Genes found in the X chromosome. Examples are the genes for hemophilia and color blindness, which affect males chiefly.

SOL - A substance that consists chiefly of a liquid such as water in which are dispersed many particles of limited size (1/1000 micron to 1/10 micron); protoplasm may be a sol.

SPAWNING - The shedding of eggs and milt into the water during the reproductive process of fish.

SPERMATOPHYTES - Phylum of seed plants.

SPHINCTER - A ringlike muscle like the one at the opening of the stomach into the small intestine.

SPIRACLES - Breathing pores of insects.

SPIRILLAE - Cork-screw shaped bacteria.

SPIROGYRA - A filamentous alga common in pond scum.

SPORE - A single-celled (occasionally two-celled) reproductive body, formed sexually or non-sexually, with or without a resistant wall, produced by plants and some protozoa.

SPOROPHYTE - In an alternation of generations, the plant that produces asexual spores.

STAMEN - The male organ of the flower, in which the pollen is made.

STAMINATE FLOWERS - Flowers that contain stamens but no pistils.

STAPHYLOCOCCUS - Certain round bacteria that often form clusters like bunches of grapes; called staph, for short.

STIGMA - The top of a pistil; here the pollen germinates.

STOMATE - Opening in the epidermis of a plant leaf through which there is an exchange of gases between the air spaces and the outside atmosphere.

STYLE - The stem of a pistil.

SUCCESSION - A series of changing plant (or animal) population at a given location; example: lichens, mosses, ferns, herbs, shrubs, poplars, pines, oaks, beech-maple climax.

SYMBIONTS - Different organisms living intimately together to the advantage of both.

SYMBIOSIS - A partnership between two dissimilar organisms in which they live intimately together and help each other, as the alga and fungus partnership in a lichen.

SYMPATHIN - A neurohumor, now usually called ADRENALIN.

SYNAPSE - The point at which a nerve impulse passes from one person into another.

SYSTEM - A group of organs cooperating to do one big job. For example, the digestive, breathing, nervous, and circulatory systems.

T

TELOPHASE - Last stage in mitosis during which two new nuclei are formed and two new cells formed from one.

TERRACING - A method of farming used on steep hillsides. Reduces erosion by catching water in ditches.

THALLOPHYTES - Lowest phylum of the plant kingdom, including algae and fungi.

THIAMIN - The chemical which is called vitamin B1. Prevents beriberi.

THROMBOKINASE - Substances released from injured cells and brokendown blood platelets which change prothrombin to thrombin if calcium ions are present.

THYROXIN - The hormone made by the thyroid gland. Rich in iodine. Helps the body burn food.

TISSUE - A group of similar cells doing the same work, such as nerve, bone, blood, or muscle tissue.

TRANSPIRATION - The loss of water by evaporation, mostly through the stomates of the leaves of a plant.

TRILOBITE - A fossilized primitive arthropod found in abundance in Paleozoic rocks; extinct by the end of the Paleozoic Era.

TROPISM - The turning of an organism away from or toward a stimulus; a positive tropism is toward; a negative tropism is away from.

TRYPTOPHAN - An amino acid that is essential in man and other animals.

TUBER - A short underground stem used as a storage organ, as the Irish potato.

U

ULOTHRIX - A genus of algae.

USE-AND-DISUSE THEORY - Lammarck's theory of evolution, now discarded.

V

VACCINE - A substance consisting of dead or weakened bacteria or viruses. Used to produce immunity in people and animals.

VACUOLE - A tiny cavity inside a plant or animal cell. Filled with liquid.

VAGUS NERVES - The pair of cranial nerves which supply the heart, stomach, and other organs.

VEINS - Blood vessels which carry blood back toward the heart.

VENTRAL - The lower or front side of an animal.

VENTRICLES - The two thick-walled chambers of the heart.

VERTEBRATES - Animals which have a backbone. Include fish, frogs, snakes, birds, deer, and man.

VESTIGIAL ORGAN - A remnant of a once useful organ, as toe bones in a bird's wing.

VILLUS - Tiny, finger-like projections on the walls of the small intestine. Absorb digested foods.

W

WHITE BLOOD COUNT - A count of the white blood cells in a cubic millimeter of blood; a procedure much used in diagnosing appendicitis and other acute infections.

WIDE CROSSING - The practice of crossing two very different animals. For example: a lion with a tigress, or a horse with a zebra.

X-Y-Z

X-CHROMOSOME - One of a pair of chromosomes that controls the sex of the individual. Females have two X-chromosomes.

XEROPHYTES - Plants that grow in very dry conditions, such as the cactus.

XYLEM - Wood cells which serve as passageways for water in the roots, stems, and leaves of ferns and seed plants.

Y-CHROMOSOME - Chromosome found in males only. Males have one X-chromosome and one Y-chromosome.

ZOOSPORE - A spore that can swim, as in ulothrix

CHEMICAL NOTES AND RESOURCES

TABLE OF CONTENTS

	Page
GLOSSARY OF CHEMICAL TERMS	
Absolute temperature ... Alkali	1
Alkylation ... Aniline	2
Anion ... Base	3
Base-formers ... Carat	4
Carbogen ... Chemical Equilibrium	5
Chemical Symbol ... Concentrated	6
Condensation ... DDT	7
Decomposition Reactions ... Drier	8
Dross ... Emulsifier	9
Emulsion ... Exposure	10
Exothermic ... Formula Weight	11
Fourdrinier Machine ... Heat of Formation	12
Heat of Neutralization ... Inert Substance	13
Inhibitor ... Kindling Temperature	14
Kinetic Energy ... Mass Action (Law Of)	15
Matte ... Monoclinic	16
Monomer ... Nitrogen Cycle	17
Nitrogen Fixation ... Oxidation	18
Oxygen-Carbon Dioxide Cycle ... Pickling	19
Pigment ... Proteins	20
Proton ... Resin	21
Rhombic ... Solder	22
Solubility Product Constant ... Supersaturated	23
Surface-Active Agent ... Thermoplastic Type of Plastics	24
Thermosetting Type of Plastics ... Vapor Tension	25
Vat Dyes ... Wetting Agents	26
X-Rays ... Zirconium	27
CHEMICAL LAWS	
Avogadro's Hypothesis ... Law of Conservation of Energy	27
Law of Conservation of Matter (Mass) ... Periodic Law (Moseley's)	28
GLOSSARY OF COMMON SUBSTANCES	
Alum ... Carbonic Acid Gas	29
Caustic potash ... Hypo	30
Kaolin ... Quicksilver	31
Rochelle Salt ... Zinc White	32
CHEMICAL ELEMENTS AND SYMBOLS	
Actinium ... Lanthanum	33
Lead ... Tungsten	34
Uranium ... Zirconium	35
PERIODIC TABLE OF THE ELEMENTS	36

CHEMICAL NOTES AND RESOURCES
GLOSSARY OF CHEMICAL TERMS

A

ABSOLUTE TEMPERATURE

Temperature on the Absolute scale whose zero is -273Centigrade.

ABSORPTION

A soaking up throughout the mass.

ACCELERATOR

Chemical additive which hastens or increases the speed of a chemical reaction. Used, for example, to improve the vulcanization of natural and synthetic rubber and latex compounds.

ACID

A water soluble chemical compound containing hydrogen replaceable by metals or basic radicals. An acid reacts with an alkali to form a salt and water. Example of acid: sulfuric acid, commonly used in storage batteries and many other applications.

ACID ANHYDRIDE

An oxide of a nonmetal capable of uniting with water to form an acid.

ACID-FORMERS

A property usually characteristic of those elements called nonmetals.

ACID SALT

A salt containing replaceable hydrogen.

ACID SULFITE

A salt formed by the union of a metal with the HSO ion.

ACRILAN

One of the synthetic fibers.

ADSORPTION

A condensation on the surface of a material.

ADSORPTION, ACTIVATED

That form of adsorption in which sufficient heat energy must be supplied before the film forms. This process is probably chemical in nature.

AERATED

Given an opportunity to dissolve or combine with air or some other gas.

AEROSOLS

Fog-like sprays.

AIR-SLAKED LIME

A mixture of calcium hydroxide and calcium carbonate formed by exploding calcium hydroxide to the air.

ALCOHOL

A compound containing an organic radical and one or more OH groups.

ALDEHYDE

An organic compound containing the CHO group.

ALIPHATIC

(Derived from Greek word for fat.) Pertaining to an open chain carbon compound. Usually applied to petroleum products derived from a paraffin base and having a straight or branched chain, saturated or unsaturated, molecular structure as distinguished from aromatic hydrocarbons which are built up from one or more benzene rings. Gasoline is a typical aliphatic hydrocarbon.

ALKALI

A compound that has the power to neutralize an acid and form a salt. Example: sodium hydroxide, referred to as caustic soda or lye. Used in soap manufacture and many other applications.

ALKYLATION
A process for rearranging straight chain hydrocarbons.

ALLOTROPISM
The ability of some elements to exist in more than one form.

ALLOY
A material composed of two or more metals.

ALPHA PARTICLES
Positively charged helium nuclei.

ALUM
The double sulfate of a monovalent and trivalent metal, containing a definite amount of water of hydration ($KAl(SO_4)_2 \cdot 12 H_2O$).

ALUMINOTHERMY
A thermite or similar reaction.

AMALGAM
An alloy of mercury with one or more other metals.

AMALGAMATION PROCESS
A process of extracting gold from ore by amalgamating the gold with mercury.

AMINO ACIDS
The "building blocks" from which the giant protein molecules are constructed.

AMMONIA (NH_3)
Nitrogen and hydrogen compound, a colorless gas liquefied by compression. Dissolves in water to form aqueous ammonia. Synthetic ammonia is main source of nitrogen for fertilizer and chemical production.

AMMONIUM ION. NH_4^+
This is a cation produced by the ionization of an ammonium salt.

AMMONIUM RADICAL, NH_4
An ammonium radical is a group of atoms which plays the role of a metal in certain salts (e.g., NH_4Cl).

AMORPHOUS
This is a substance without crystalline structure. The atoms or molecules are not arranged in a definite pattern.

AMPERE
An Ampere is one coulomb of electricity per second. That current which deposits .00III8g. silver per second.

AMPHOTERIC
Referring to a compound which may ionize as a base in the presence of a strong acid, and as an acid in the presence of a strong base.

ANGSTROM UNIT (A)
$= 10^{-8}$ cm.

ANHYDRIDE
A compound, usually an oxide of a metal or a nonmetal, capable of uniting with water to form a base or an acid.

ANHYDROUS
Material from which the water has been removed.

ANILINE ($C_6H_5NH_2$)
One of the most important of organics derived from coal. Building block for many dyes and drugs.

ANION

An anion is a negatively charged ion. It is attracted to the anode (+electrode) during electrolysis.

ANODE

The positive terminal of an electric cell.

ANTIBIOTIC

A substance either synethesized chemically or produced by a microorganism, usually a mold or fungus, which kills other organisms, or retards, or completely represses their growth, normally without harm to higher orders of life. Antibiotics retain highly germicidial properties even in dilute concentrations.

ANTICHLOR

A chemical which acts against chlorine, such as a solution of sodium thiosulfate.

ANTIOXIDANT

A compound added to rubber and other substances to prevent deterioration by oxidation.

AQUA AMMONIA

A solution of ammonia gas in water.

AQUA REGIA

A mixture of concentrated nitric and hydrochloric acids capable of dissolving gold.

ARC-TYPE FURNACE

One that has an electric arc jumping the gap between carbon electrodes.

AROMATIC

Applied to group of hydrocarbons derived from or characterized by presence of the benzene nucleus (molecular ring structure). Sometimes called "cyclic solvents" or "cyclic hydrocarbons."

ASSOCIATION

A joining together of small molecules to form larger molecules.

ATOM

A chemical unit, the smallest part of an element which remains unchanged during any chemical reaction yet may undergo physical changes to other atoms as in atomic fission. Believed to be made up of a complex system whose electrically charged components are in rapid orbital motion.

ATOMIC NUMBER

A number identifying an element, equal to the number of protons in its atoms.

ATOMIC WEIGHT

The average relative weight of the atoms of an element compared with those of oxygen taken as a standard and given a value of 16.

<u>B</u>

BACITRACIN

One of the newer antibiotics.

BAKING SODA

The compound sodium hydrogen carbonate used in baking powders and for other purposes

BAROMETER

An apparatus for measuring atmospheric pressure.

BASE

A compound containing the hydroxyl group which, when dissolved in water, forms no negative ions but hydroxyl ions.

BASE-FORMERS
A property usually characteristic of metals.
BASIC ANHYDRIDE
An oxide of a metal capable of reacting with water to form a base. **BASIC SALT**
A salt containing replaceable oxygen or hydroxyl groups.
BENZENE (C_6H_6)
Major organic intermediate derived from coal or petroleum. Ring-shaped (cyclic) molecular structure makes it broadly useful as chemical building block.
BESSEMER CONVERTER
An egg-shaped converter which changes pig iron into steel by burning out impurities with an air blast.
BETA PARTICLES
Negatively charged particles, actually electrons, emitted by some radioactive materials.
BETATRON
One of the types of "atom-smashing" machines for bombarding atomic nuclei.
BINARY
Binary compounds are made up of only two elements.
BISQUE
A porous porcelain product that has been fired only once.
BLOCK TIN
Solid tin, as distinguished from tin-plate.
BOILING POINT
The temperature at which the vapor pressure of a liquid reaches atmospheric pressure.
BOTTLED GAS
Propane, butane, or a mixture of both, stored under pressure in steel cylinders and used as a fuel.
BREEDER REACTOR
A reactor which uses some fissionable material to produce energy and a greater quantity of fissionable material.
BRITISH THERMAL UNIT (B.T.U.)
The quantity of heat necessary to raise the temperature of one pound of water one degree Fahrenheit.
BROWNIAN MOVEMENT
The zigzag movement of colloidal particles through the medium in which they are suspended.
BUFFER
A suitable mixture of salt and acid (or salt and base) that regulates or stabilizes the pH of a solution.

<u>C</u>

CALCINE
A partially refined copper ore.
CALORIE
A unit for measuring heat, equal to the amount of heat necessary to raise one gram of water one degree Centigrade.
CALORIMETER
A vessel used in measuring the heat evolved in chemical or physical changes.
CARAT
A unit of weight used for gems, equal to 200 milligrams.

CARBOGEN

A mixture of oxygen with 5% to 10% of carbon dioxide.

CARBOHYDRATES

Compounds containing carbon, hydrogen, and oxygen, usually with the hydrogen and oxygen present in the ratio of two to one.

CARBONATED BEVERAGES

Beverages which contain dissolved carbon dioxide.

CARBOXYL

The COOH group in organic compounds as found in organic acids.

CARBURETOR

The second or middle chamber of a water gas apparatus in which the gas is often enriched by spraying in oil or by adding propane.

CATALYST

A substance which through acceleration or retardation changes the spread of a chemical reaction and effects a definite change in composition and/or properties of the end product. In paint manufacture, catalysts generally become part of the final product. In most uses, however, they do not.

CATHODE

The negative electrode or terminal.

CATION

(1) A positively charged ion. (2) The ion attracted to the cathode in electrolysis.

CAUSTIC

A substance that attacks skin, hair, or such materials by chemical action.

CELLULOSE ($C_5H_{10}O_{5n}$)

A carbohydrate which makes up the structural material of vegetable tissues and fibers. Purest forms: chemical cotton and chemical pulp. Basis of rayon, acetate and cellophane.

CEMENT

A mixture made from limestone and clay which, after mixing with water, sets to a hard mass.

CEMENTATION

A process formerly used for making steel by heating wrought iron in red-hot charcoal for a long period of time.

CENTIGRADE TEMPERATURE

Temperature on the Centigrade scale which has $0°$ for the freezing point of water and $100°$ for the boiling point at a pressure of 760 mm.

CHAIN REACTION

A reaction in which the material or energy which starts the reaction is also a product.

CHAMBER PROCESS

A process for making sulfuric acid in large lead chambers, using oxides of nitrogen to promote the necessary reaction.

CHECKERWORK

Loosely-stacked firebricks in a chamber providing a circuitous passage for fuel gas or air.

CHEMICAL CHANGE

A change which produces a new substance with new properties.

CHEMICAL EQUATION

A qualitative and quantitative expression of a chemical change.

CHEMICAL EQUILIBRIUM

A reaction in which the products unite to form the original reactants at the same speed at which the reactants are forming the product.

CHEMICAL SYMBOL
Either one or two letters used as an abbreviation for an element.

CHEMOTHERAPY
Use of chemicals of particular molecular structure in the treatment of specific disorders on the assumption that known structures exhibit an affinity for certain parts of cells of affected tissues and thereby eliminate the causative factors.

CHEMURGY
That branch of applied chemistry devoted to industrial utilization of organic raw materials, especially farm products, as in the use of pine tree cellulose for rayon and paper, and soy bean oil for paints and varnishes.

CHLORINATION
Adding chlorine to a material.

CHLOROMYCETIN
One of the antibiotics.

CHLOROPHYLL
Green coloring matter in leaves which acts as a catalyst for photosynthesis.

CHLORTETRACYCLINE
One of the antibiotics, formerly called aureomycin.

CHROMOPHORS
Certain groups whose presence results in compounds having a color.

COAL GAS
A fuel gas obtained by the destructive distillation of soft coal.

COKE OVEN CHEMICALS
Those organic compounds derived from bituminous coal in the production of metallurgical coke. This major chemical raw materials source provides a base for thousands of chemicals.

COLLOID
A particle in an extremely fine state of subdivision.

COMBINATION REACTIONS
Those in which one element reacts with another to form a compound.

COMBINING WEIGHT
The number of grams of an element that will combine with or replace 8 grams of oxygen or its equivalent.

COMBUSTION
Oxidation accompanied by noticeable light and heat.

COMMON-ION EFFECT
The addition of a substance containing an ion common to that already present, causing the reaction to be driven in a definite direction.

COMPONENT
One of a minimum number of substances necessary to give the composition of a system.

COMPOST
A product of the decay of plant material.

COMPOUND
A substance composed of two or more elements joined according to the laws of chemical combination. Each compound has its own characteristic properties different from those of its elements.

CONCENTRATED
Containing much of a material, the opposite of dilute.

CONDENSATION
(1) Changing a material such as vapor to a liquid;
(2) Increasing the size of very small particles up to colloidal size;
(3) A reaction between raw materials in the making of a plastic that results in the formation of water as one of the products.

CONTACT PROCESS
A process for making sulfuric acid in which the sulfur dioxide and oxygen come in contact with a catalyst.

COORDINATE VALENCE
A kind of chemical bonding somewhat similar to co-valence, but in which there is only one donor atom.

CORTISONE
A compound of animal origin, used particularly for athritis.

COSMIC RAYS
These are rays which come to the earth from somewhere in space, perhaps beyond the solar system.

COTTRELL PRECIPITATOR
A device for precipitating colloidal dust with electricity of high voltage.

COUNTERCURRENTS
Two currents proceeding in opposite directions through an apparatus.

COVALENCE
A kind of chemical bonding in which two atoms share an electron with each other. C.P. Abbreviation for "chemically pure."

CRACKING
Breaking large or complex molecules into simpler, smaller molecules.

CRITICAL PRESSURE
The pressure of a system at its critical temperature.

CRITICAL SIZE
The smallest amount of fissionable material which can sustain a chain reaction.

CRITICAL TEMPERATURE
The highest temperature at which a liquid and its vapor can co-exist as separate phases.

CRYSTALLOID
A term applied to materials that crystallize easily and pass through a semi-permeable membrane without difficulty.

CRYSTALS
Solids separated from solutions having a definite shape or structure.

GULLET
Broken glass that is re-melted with raw materials in a new batch of glass.

CUPELLATION
A process of separating gold and silver from a base metal such as lead. An oxidizing flame converts the lead to the oxide (PbO), which is removed by a stream of air or is absorbed in the porous bottom of the reverberatory furnace. The silver-gold residue remains unchanged.

CYCLOTRON
One of the atom-smashing machines used to bombard the nuclei of atoms.

D

DACRON
One of the synthetic fibers.

DDT
Letters stand for dichloro-diphenyl-trichloroethane, an insecticide.

DECOMPOSITION REACTIONS
Those in which a compound is decomposed by heat, light, or electricity into simpler compounds.

DECREPITATION
The expulsion of water with a crackling sound when some crystals are heated.

DEHYDRATION
The removal of water from a substance.

DELIQUESCENCE
The process of picking up enough water to become wet.

DENSITY
Mass per unit volume, e.g., grams per cubic centimeter.

DESTRUCTIVE DISTILLATION
The process of heating wood, coal, bones, etc., in a closed vessel, resulting in a breaking down to simpler materials.

DETERGENT
An agent that removes dirt.

DEUTERIUM
An isotope of hydrogen of mass 2.

DEUTERON
The nucleus of the deuterium atom.

DEVELOPING
A process in photography in which the reduction of the silver compound, started by light, is promoted by the action of an alkaline, organic, reducing agent.

DIALYSIS
A process in which a semi-permeable membrane is used to separate colloidal particles from substances in true solution.

DIBASIC
A term applied to acids that have two replaceable hydrogen atoms.

DIESELENE
A petroleum fuel for Diesel engines.

DIFFUSION
The intermingling of liquids and gases.

DILUENT
A diluting agent, such as water in a solution, or turpentine in paint.

DIPOLES
Molecules with unbalanced charges so that one end may be positive and the other end negative.

DISINFECTANTS
Agents that kill, not merely arrest, the growth of bacteria.

DISSOCIATION
The separation of the ions of an electrovalent compound by the action of a solvent.

DISTILLATION
The process of evaporation followed by condensation of the vapors in a separate vessel.

DOUBLE REPLACEMENT REACTIONS
Those in which two compounds exchange ions to produce two new compounds.

DOUBLE SALT
A salt in which two metal atoms are combined with one acid radical or one metal is combined with two acid radicals, e.g., $KAl(SO_4)_2 \; 12 \; H_2O$.

DRIER
Catalysts, such as oxides of lead and manganese, added to paint to promote the drying of the paint.

DROSS
A powdery scum that floats on top of melted metal.

DUCTILITY
That property of a substance which permits its being drawn into wire.

DUTCH PROCESS
A process for making white lead using lead buckles, acetic acid, and decomposing tanbark or manure.

DYNAMITE
An explosive made by absorbing nitroglycerin in wood flour mixed with sodium nitrate.

DYNE
A unit of force. The force necessary to give a mass of one gram an acceleration of one centimeter per second per second.

DYNEL
One of the synthetic fibers.

EFFERVESCENCE
The process of giving off bubbles of gas from a liquid.

EFFLORESCENCE
The property of giving off water vapor to the air.

ELASTOMER
Actually, it is any flexible or elastic material but, in a more limited sense, a synthetic rubber or soft or rubbery plastic with some degree of elasticity at room temperature.

ELECTRIC POTENTIAL
Electrical pressure or voltage between terminals.

ELECTRODE
A terminal of an electric circuit where the current either enters or leaves.

ELECTROLYTE
A compound whose water solution conducts an electric current.

ELECTRON
A unit particle of negative electricity. Its mass is 1/1845 of the hydrogen atom.

ELECTRON VOLT
That quantity of energy which is equal to the kinetic energy of an electron accelerated by a potential difference of 1 volt.

ELECTRONEGATIVE ELEMENT
An element which has a tendency to take up electrons.

ELECTROPLATING
Deposition of metals on a surface by means of an electric current.

ELECTROTYPES
Copper plates from which the pages of a book are printed.

ELECTROVALENCE
Type of chemical bonding where one or more electrons are transferred from one atom to another.

ELEMENT
Solid, liquid or gaseous matter consisting of atoms of one type which cannot be further decomposed by chemical means. The atoms of an element may differ physically but do not differ chemically. Example: chlorine. Known elements: 101.

EMULSIFIER, EMULSIFYING AGENT
A chemical that mixes and disperses dissimilar materials to produce an emulsion and keep it stable. Casein, for example is a natural emulsi-fier in milk, keeping butter fat droplets emulsified.

EMULSION
Suspension of insoluble fine particles or globules of a liquid in another liquid.

ENDOTHERMIC
Pertaining to a reaction which absorbs heat.

ENERGY
The capacity for doing work.

ENZYME
An organic secretion that acts as a catalyst.

EQUATION
An expression which shows, by the use of symbols and formulas, the changes in arrangement of the atoms which occur during a chemical reaction.

EQUILIBRIUM
A reaction in which the products unite to form the original reactants at the same speed at which the reactants are forming the products.

EQUILIBRIUM (CHEMICAL)
A state in which a chemical reaction and the reverse reaction are taking place at the same rate. The concentrations (at equilibrium) of all substances remain constant.

EQUILIBRIUM CONSTANT
An equilibrium constant (K) is the ratio (number) obtained by dividing the product of the active concentrations of the substances produced in a reaction by the product of the active concentrations of the reactants, after equilibrium has been reached.

ERG
The work done by a force of one dyne per centimeter.

ESTER
A compound formed by the reaction between an acid and an alcohol.

ESTERIFICATION
The process of preparing esters by adding acid to an alcohol

ETHANE (C_2H_6)
A saturated hydrocarbon (maximum number of hydrogen atoms attached to each carbon) derived from petroleum or natural gas, important for organic synthesis. Ethylene derived from it.

ETHANOL (ETHYL ALCOHOL) (C_2H_5OH)
Organic compound derived through either a fermentation process or via synthesis from petroleum or natural gas. Wide use as solvent and for chemical synthesis.

ETHYLENE (C_2H_4)
Gaseous organic compound prepared in cracking of petroleum or by passing natural gas through heated tube. Removal of two hydrogen atoms from ethane component of petroleum or natural gas makes this unsaturated hydrocarbon of wide use as petrochemical base for numerous chemical reactions, notably plastic material manufacture.

ETHYLENE GLYCOL
Colorless liquid which is a useful humectant since it absorbs approximately twice its weight of water at room temperature and 100% humidity. A major use: anti-freeze. Among many other uses -chemical synthesis, as in producing alkyd resins.

EUTECTIC
A mixture of two or more substances with the lowest melting point.

EXPLOSIVE RANGE
A pair of percentages below or above which the gas will not form an explosive mixture with air.

EXPOSURE
In photography, the act of admitting light to the film or plate.

EXOTHERMIC
Pertaining to a reaction which liberates heat.
EXTRUDED
Forced through a die by pressure.

F

FAHRENHEIT TEMPERATURE
Temperature on the Fahrenheit scale with 32° as the freezing point of water and 212° as the boiling point at a pressure of 760 mm.
FAMILY OF ELEMENTS
A group of elements with more or less similar properties.
FATS
Glyceryl esters of certain organic acids.
FELDSPARS
Complex silicates, usually aluminum silicate with either sodium or potassium silicate.
FERMENTATION
A chemical reaction caused by living organisms or enzymes.
FERTILIZER
Plant food, or material, that contains compounds of the elements needed by plants for growth.
FILTRATION
The process of removing suspended material from a liquid by allowing the liquid to pass through a material such as filter paper or a layer of sand.
FISSION
The disintegration of an atom into two nyclei with nearly equal mass.
FIXATION OF NITROGEN
A process in which atmospheric nitrogen is converted into useful compounds.
FIXING
In photography the operation of removing unchanged silver salts after the picture has been developed, thereby fixing the image on the film or plate.
FLOTATION (ORE)
A process in which crushed ore is agitated in water containing a fro-ther (pine oil) and a collector (potassium ethyl xanthate). The valuable mineral particles are attached to the froth and rise to the surface from which they are removed.
FLOTATION REAGENT
Chemical used in flotation separation of minerals. Added to pulverized mixture of solids, water and oil, causes preferential oil-wetting of certain solid particles, making possible the flotation and separation of un-wet particles.
FLUIDITY
The reciprocal of viscosity.
FLUORESCENT
Giving off light after exposure to sunlight.
FLOWERS OF SULFUR
Finely-divided sulfur formed by the condensation of sulfur vapors on a cool surface.
FLUX
A material added to unite with impurities to form an easily melted product.
FORMULA
A collection of chemical symbols indicating what elements and how many atoms of each are present in a compound.
FORMULA WEIGHT
The sum of the weights of the atoms in a formula.

FOURDRINIER MACHINE
A machine that converts a suspension of taper fibers into sheets.
FRACTIONAL CRYSTALLIZATION
Separation of two dissolved solids by evaporating until the less soluble solid separates while the more soluble solid remains in solution.
FRACTIONATION
The process of separating a mixture by careful evaporation, depending upon the materials having different boiling points.
FROTH-FLOTATION
A process for concentrating powdered ore by causing the good ore to cling to bubbles which float above liquid, while the worthless rocky material sinks to the bottom of the container.
FUNGICIDE
Any one of a group of chemicals used to prevent or inhibit the growth of fungi or bacteria. Among these are: plant fungicides, wood preservatives, mildew or mold preventives and disinfectants.

G

GALVANIZE
To coat iron or steel with zinc.
GAMMA RAYS
High energy X-rays emitted from a radioactive material.
GANGUE
Worthless material, rock or earth, present in an ore.
GEIGER COUNTER
A device used to detect the presence of radiation from radioactive material.
GEL
A jelly-like solid.
GENERATOR
In chemistry, the vessel in which a reaction occurs between chemicals.
GERMAN SILVER
An alloy containing copper, nickel, and zinc.
GRAM
Basic unit of weight in the metric system, equal to 1/1000 of the standard kilogram.
GRAM-EQUIVALENT WEIGHT
The weight of an element that will combine with or replace one gram of hydrogen.
GRAM-FORMULA WEIGHT
The number of grams of a substance that equal its formula weight.
GRAM-MOLECULAR VOLUME
The volume, 22.4 liters, occupied by one gram-molecular weight at any gast at S.T.P.
GRAM-MOLECULAR WEIGHT
That number of grams of any substance that equal its molecular weight, also called a MOLE of that substance

H

HALF-LIFE
The time required for one-half the atoms of a mass of radioactive material to decompose.
HALOGEN
The name given to the family of elements having seven valence electrons.
HEAT OF FORMATION
The heat which is given out or absorbed when a compound is formed from elements.

HEAT OF NEUTRALIZATION
The number of calories liberated in the formation of 18g. of water from hydrogen and hydroxyl ions.

HEAVY WATER
Water containing deuterium atoms in place of ordinary hydrogen atoms.

HEMOGLOBIN
The red coloring matter in blood.

HERBICIDE
A weed-killing agent. Most of these are specific in their action and therefore not intended for indiscriminate use. Label indicates particular purposes and gives directions for most effective application.

HOMOLOGOUS SERIES
A series of compounds each of which can be represented by a type of formula, such as C_nH_{2n+2}.

HUMIDITY, RELATIVE
The ratio of the actual amount of water vapor in atmosphere to the amount necessary for saturation at the same temperature.

HYDRATE
Crystals that contain water of hydration.

HYDRATED LIME
Calcium hydroxide, the product formed when water unites with calcium oxide.

HYDROCARBONS
Organic compounds composed solely of caron and hydrogen. Myriad variety of molecular combinations of C and H. Basic building block of all organic chemicals. Main chemical industry course of hydrocarbons: petroleum, natural gas and coal.

HYDROFORMING
The process of improving gasoline by heating it with hydrogen in the presence of a catalyst.

HYDROGENATION
The addition of hydrogen to a material.

HYDROLYSIS
The reaction of water with a salt to form the acid and the base of which the salt was a product; it opposes neutralization reactions.

HYDROPONICS
The science of gardening without the use of oil.

HYGROSCOPIC
Having a tendency to pick up water vapor.

I

INACTIVE SUBSTANCE
One which reacts, but not very readily, with other substances.

INDICATOR
A substance used to show, by means of a color change, whether an acid or a base is present.

INERT ELEMENT
An element of the zero group of the periodic table. Elements in this group have no chemical properties.

INERT SUBSTANCE
One which does not react at all with other substances under the usual conditions of chemical reactions.

INHIBITOR
(1) A material used to prevent or retard rust or corrosion.
(2) An agent which arrests or slows chemical action.

INORGANIC
Term used to designate chemicals that generally do not contain carbon. Source: matter, other than vegetable or animal. Example: chlorine is an inorganic chemical derived from salt.

INSECTICIDE
Any one of a group of chemicals used to kill or control insects.

INTERMEDIATE
An organic chemical formed as a "middle-step" between the initial material and the one or frequently several ultimate end products.

INVERSION
The combination of cane sugar with water to form two molecules of simple sugars.

ION
An atom or group of atoms which carries an electric charge.

ION-EXCHANGE RESINS
Granules of resins that absorb either positive or negative ions.

IONIC EQUILIBRIUM
The balance attained when the rate of dissociation equals the rate of association.

IOOTZATION
The formation of ions from polar compounds by action of a solvent.

IONIZATION CONSTANT
The product of the concentration of the ions divided by the concentration of the unionized molecules of solute (electrolyte).

IONIZATION POTENTIAL
The energy necessary to remove an electron from a gaseous atom to form an ion. This energy is expressed in electron volts.

IRRADIATION
Subjected to light, especially ultraviolet light.

ISOBARES
Atoms of the same atomic weight but having different atomic numbers are isobares.

ISOMERS
Compounds having the same composition but different structure.

ISOTOPE
One of two or more atomic species of an element differing in weight but having the same nuclear charge (atomic number). For example, in the element, chlorine, the atomic weight is the mean of the two isotopes making up the element.

K

KAOLIN
A fine, white clay composed of hydrated aluminum silicate.

KERNEL
All of the atom except the valence electrons.

KILN
A type of furnace used for producing quicklime, making glass, baking pottery, etc.

KILOCALORIES
Units equal to one thousand calories.

KILOGRAM
The standard of weight in the metric system equal to 1000 grams.

KINDLING TEMPERATURE
The lowest temperature at which a substance takes fire. This temperature varies with the physical state of the substance.

KINETIC ENERGY
Energy of motion.

KINETIC THEORY
The theory of matter which assumes that all molecules of matter are always in motion.

KNOCKING
A pounding sound produced in automobile engines by too rapid combustion of the mixture of gasoline vapor and air.

L

LAC OF SULPHUR
Precipitated sulfur.

LATENT HEAT
The heat absorbed or liberated in changing a mole of substance from one state to another at a fixed temperature, e.g., converting 18g. water to water vapor at $100°$ C.

LATEX
Original meaning: Milky extract from rubber tree. Now also applied to water emulsions of synthetic rubbers or resins. In emulsion paints, the film-forming resin is in the form of latex.

LAW, LeCHATELIER'S
A system in equilibrium, if disturbed by external factors such as temperature and pressure, will adjust itself in such a way that the effect of the disturbing factors will be reduced to a minimum.

LEHR
A cooling oven for annealing glass.

LIGNIN
Major non-carbohydrate constituent of wood and woody plants; functions as binder for the cellulose fibers. Removed from wood in pulp manufacture. Extracted from waste sulfite liquor. Research underway on chemical applications. Current use as adhesive base, for boiler water treatment and for road binders.

LIGNITE
A partially mineralized peat.

LIME
A term loosely used for all calcium compounds but properly belonging to calcium oxide, although often used for calcium hydroxide and calcium carbonate.

L.P.G., or LIQUEFIED PETROLEUM GAS
A compressed or liquefied gas comprised of pure propane, or a butane, or a combination of propane and butane; obtained as a by-product in petroleum refining or gasoline manufacture. Used in chemical synthesis.

LITER
The basic unit of volume in the metric system.

LITHOPANE
A paint base composed of barium sulfate and zinc sulfide.

LITMUS
A dye extracted from lichens which is used as an indicator.

LYE
A term used for either sodium hydroxide or potassium hydroxide.

M

MASS
The property of a substance (body) that determines the acceleration it will acquire when acted upon by a given force.

MASS ACTION, LAW OF
The speed of a chemical change is proportional to the concentration of the reacting substances.

MATTE
A mixture of sulfides produced in a partially refined ore.

MATTER
Anything which occupies space and has weight.

METALLURGY
The science of extracting and refining metals.

METALS
Elements with a luster that are good conductors of heat and electricity and are electropositive.

MERCERIZING
Treating stretched cotton with sodium hydroxide solution.

METAMORPHIC
Applied to rocks that have undergone a change in form due to heat or pressure.

METER
The basic unit of the metric system, equal to 39.37 inches.

METHANE (CH_4)
The simplest saturated hydrocarbon, chief component of most natural gas. Chemical raw material.

METHYL ALCOHOL (METHANOL, WOOD ALCOHOL) (CH_3OH)
Organic compound important for chemical synthesis; also used in denaturing alcohol; solvent and many other uses.

MILLILITER
One-thousandth of a liter.

MILK OF SULFUR
Precipitated sulfur.

MIXTURE
Two or more substances which, when combined, do not lose their identity and may be separated by mechanical means.

MODERATOR
A substance which slows down fast neutrons.

MOLAL SOLUTION
One mole of a substance dissolved in 1000g. of solvent.

MOLAR SOLUTION
One gram-molecular weight of a substance dissolved in enough solvent to make one liter of solution.

MOLE
That number of grams of a substance which is exactly equal to its molecular weight.

MOLECULAR VOLUME
The volume occupied by a mole of any gas at $0°$ C. and 760 mm pressure, e.g., 22.4 liters.

MOLECULAR WEIGHT
The sum of the weights of the atoms in a molecule.

MOLECULE
The chemical combination of two or more like or unlike atoms.

MONATOMIC
Molecules made up of one atom.

MONOBASIC ACID
An acid having one replaceable hydrogen atom per molecule.

MONOCLINIC
Referring to those crystals having one oblique axis.

MONOMER

A compound of relatively low molecular weight which, under certain conditions, either alone or with another monomer, forms various types and lengths of molecular chains called polymers or copolymers of high molecular weight. Example: styrene is a monomer which polymerizes readily to make the polymer, polystyrene.

MORTAR

A mixture of lime, sand, and water.

MOTHER LIQUOR

The liquid which is left after a crop of crystals has separated from a solution.

<u>N</u>

NAPHTHALENE ($C_{10}H_8$)

A white solid crystalline hydrocarbon found as a mineral and obtained from coal tar by distillation. Used as a moth repellent and a basic material in the manufacture of dyestuffs, synthetic resins, lubricants and other products.

NAPHTHENES

Hydrocarbons having a ring structure.

NASCENT

At the instant an element is liberated from a compound it is said to be in the nascent state. Nascent dryogen is probably atomic hydrogen.

NATIVE METAL

A metal found as an element, rather than as a compound, in the ground.

NATURAL GAS

A combustible gas composed largely of methane and other hydrocarbons with variable amounts of nitrogen and non-combustible gases; obtained from natural earth fissures or from driven wells. Among other things, used as a fuel, in the manufacture of carbon black and in chemical synthesis of many products.

NEON (Ne)

A rare gaseous element which forms no chemical compounds and is derived by fractional distillation of liquid air. Used mostly in luminescent electric tubes.

NEUTRALIZATION

The union of hydrogen ions of an acid with hydroxyl ions of a base to form water.

NEUTRON

A neutral particle found in the atom.

NIACIN ($C_6H_5O_2N$)

The anti-pellagra factor of the vitamin B complex; present in animal tissues, in fish, milk and green leafy vegetables.

NITER (KNO_3)

A white salt widely distributed in nature and formed in soils from nitrogenous organic bodies by the action of bacteria. Used in making gunpowder, medicinals and other products.

NITRIC ACID (HNO_3)

A colorless to yellowish fuming liquid with powerful corrosive properties. Manufactured by several methods, it is used in organic synthesis, in etching metals and ore flotation, in the manufacture of explosives, medicines, and other products.

NITROCELLULOSE

A powerful explosive made by treating cellulose with nitric and sul-furic acids.

NITROGATION

Adding of nitrogen compounds to the soil.

NITROGEN CYCLE

The cycle of changes through which nitrogen passes, starting with nitrates in the soil which become, in turn, plant proteins, animal proteins, dead matter, ammonia, nitrites, and then nitrates again.

NITROGEN FIXATION
Process of combining nitrogen of the atmosphere into any of the various stable chemical compounds valuable to the manufacture of fertilizers, and ammonia, among others.

NITROGLYCERIN
Glyceryl trinitrate, a powerful and sensitive explosive.

NITROUS OXIDE (NO_2)
A colorless gas of sweetish odor and taste; used as an anesthetic. Also called laughing gas.

NONELECTROLYTE
A compound whose water solution does not conduct electric current. NONMETALS
Elements that are usually poor conductors of heat and electricity and are electro-negative.

NORMAL SALT
A salt containing neither replaceable hydrogen nor hydroxyl.

NORMAL SOLUTION
A solution that contains one gram-equivalent of a substance dissolved in enough solvent to make one liter of solution.

NUCLEONS
The fundamental constituents of atomic nuclei(protons and neutrons).

O

OCCLUSION
The adsorption of gases by solids.

OCTANE RATING
A number indicating how a gasoline behaves with regard to knocking when compared with a test fuel given an arbitrary rating of 100.

OCTET
The term applied to a group of eight electrons in the highest energy levels of atoms.

ONE ATMOSPHERE
The average pressure of the atmosphere at sea level, equal to 760 mm. of mercury.

OPEN-HEARTH PROCESS
A process for making steel in a large, shallow pool.

ORBIT
The path of an electron about the nucleus of an atom.

ORGANIC
Term used to designate that group of chemicals that contain carbon. Approximately 300,000 such compounds have been identified, many occurring in nature, others produced by chemical synthesis. Sources: petroleum and coal tar by fractional distillation; soft coal and wood by destructive distillation; wood by chemical treatment; grains and fruits by fermentation; grains, vegetables and fruit by mechanical and chemical separation of starch and sugar; cotton by mechanical and chemical treatment; animals, seeds and nuts, by mechanical extraction of fats and oils.

ORLON
One of the synthetic fibers.

OSMOSIS
The passage of liquids and gases through porous membranes.

OXIDATION
Process of combining oxygen with some other substance.

OXYGEN-CARBON DIOXIDE CYCLE
The cycle of events whereby plants take in carbon dioxide and give off oxygen in photosynthesis, whereas animals take in oxygen and give off carbon dioxide in respiration.

OZONE
An allotropic form of oxygen containing three atoms per molecule.

P

PAINT BASE
The particles suspended in the oil of a paint.

PAINT VEHICLE
A quick drying oil that forms a flexible horn-like film. The paint base is suspended in this oil.

PARAFFINS, PARAFFIN SERIES (From parun affinis-small affinity)
Those hydrocarbon components of crude oil and natural gas whose molecules are saturated (i.e., carbon atoms attached to each other by single bonds) and therefore very stable. Examples: methane, ethane.

PARKERIZED
Dipped into a hot alkaline solution of sodium phosphate.

PARKES PROCESS
A method of separating silver from molten, crude lead by adding zinc.

PEPTIZATION
A breaking up of coarse particles into a finer state of subdivision.

PERIODIC TABLE
An arrangement of the elements in the order of their atomic numbers.

PH
A numerical scale that indicates the concentration of hydrogen ions in a solution; 7 is neutral, less than 7 is acid, and greater than 7 is basic.

PHENOL (C_6H_5OH)
Popularly known as carbolic acid. Important chemical intermediate intermediate derived primarily from coal tar and produced by chemical synthesis. Base for plastics, Pharmaceuticals, explosives, anti-septics, and many other end products.

PHENOLPHTHALEIN
An indicator which turns red in the presence of an excess of hydroxyl ions.

PHOSPHORS
Compounds that fluoresce under ultraviolet light.

PHOSPHORESCENCE
A faint glow similar in appearance to that emitted by phosphorus when it is exposed to the air in a dark room.

PHOTON
A unit of light (a particle of light).

PHOTOSYNTHESIS
The process by which plants build carbohydrate foods with the aid of sunlight, using carbon dioxide and water as the raw materials and chlorophyll as the catalyst.

PHYSICAL CHANGE
A change in color, size of particle, temperature, or other physical property that does not produce a new substance.

PHYSICAL EQUILIBRIUM
A condition of balance when the rate of a physical change in one direction is equal to an opposite physical change.

PICKLING
Treating a metal with acid to remove surface coatings of oxide.

PIGMENT
A substance that adds color to a mixture.

PLASTICIZERS
Organic chemicals used in modifying plastics, synthetic rubber and similar materials to give such special properties as elongation, flexibility and toughness as may be essential to their end uses.

PLASTICS
Officially defined as any one of a large and varied group of materials which consists of, or contains as an essential ingredient, an organic substance of large molecular weight; and which, while solid in the finished state, at some stage in its manufacture has been or can be formed (cast calendered, extruded, molded, etc.) into various shapes by flow - usually through application of heat and pressure singly or together. Each plastic has individual physical, chemical and electrical properties. Two basic types: thermosetting and thermoplastic. Prior to processing, plastic materials often are referred to as resins. Final form may be as film, sheet, solid, or foam; flexible or rigid.

POLAR MOLECULE
A molecule with an unsymmetrical electron distribution.

POLING
The use of green wood in the refining of copper ore to reduce the traces of copper oxide present.

POLYMER
A high molecular weight material containing a large number of repeating units. These may be hundreds or even thousands of the original molecules (monomers) which have linked together end to end. Rubber and cellulose are naturally occurring polymers. Most resins are chemically produced polymers. Polymers may be formed by polymerization or condensation. For instance, the polymer, polyethylene, is polymerized from the monomer, ethylene. An example of condensation is the production of phenol formaldehyde resins with the incidental formation of water or some simple substance.

POLYMERIZATION
A physical reaction by which polymers are formed from the linkage of monomers.

POLYMORPHISM
The ability to exist in two or more crystalline forms.

PORCELAIN
A product made from pure, white clay mixed with powdered feldspar and usually fired twice in a kiln.

POSITRON
A unit charge of positive electricity of approximately the same mass as the electron.

POTASH
Source of potassium, essential plant nutrient (other two basic nutrients: nitrogen, phosphorus). Potash value in a fertilizer is expressed in terms of equivalent amount of potassium oxide K_2O.

PRECIPITATE
An insoluble solid formed by adding one solution to another.

PRODUCER GAS
A cheap fuel gas for industrial purposes made by blowing a blast of steam and air through red-hot coke.

PROPERTIES
The characteristics by which we identify materials.

PROTEINS
Complex organic compounds necessary for the growth of living things or the repair of worn-out tissue.

PROTON
A positively charged particle found in the atom.

Q

QUICKLIME
Calcium oxide, often called unslaked lime.

R

RADICAL
A group of atoms which acts like a single atom in forming compounds.

RADIOACTIVITY
Emission of energy in waves or moving particles from the nucleus of an atom. Always involves change of one kind of atom into a different kind. A few elements such as radium are naturally radioactive. Other radiactive forms are induced (see RADIOISOTOPE).

RADIOCHEMICALS
Any compound or mixture containing a sufficient portion of radioactive elements to be detected by Geiger counter.

RADIOISOTOPE
An isotopic form of an element that exhibits radioactivity, whether naturally found or produced by fission and other induced nuclear changes. The latter are used in biological tracer work and industrial control operations. More than 500 radioactive substances have been produced.

RADON
A gaseous element produced by the disintegration of radium atoms.

REACTANTS
The elements or compounds entering into a chemical reaction.

REAGENT
Any substance used in a chemical reaction to produce another substance or to detect its composition.

REDOX REACTION
A reaction in which oxidation and reduction take place.

REDUCING AGENT
An agent that removes oxygen from a material.

REDUCTION
(1) Removal of oxygen. (2) The gain in electrons by an element.

REFRACTORY
Pertaining to a substance that is not easily melted.

REGENERATIVE HEATING
A system whereby the heat of outgoing flue gases is used to preheat incoming fuel gas and air.

RELATIVE HUMIDITY
The amount of moisture present in the air as a vapor compared with the total amount of moisture the air could hold at that temperature.

REPLACEMENT SERIES
The arrangement of the metals in the order of their decreasing chemical activity.

RESIN
A solid or semisolid amorphous organic compound or mixture of such compounds with no definite melting point and no tendency to crystallize. Resins may be of vegetable, animal or synthetic origin. Natural resins may be distinguished from gums in that they are insoluble in water. However, certain synthetic water soluble materials are referred to as resins or resin

stages. There are many types, each with distinctive physical and chemical properties. Some types of resin materials may be molded, cast, or extruded. Others are used for adhesives, for the treatment of textiles and paper, and for protective coatings. Still others are rolled or extruded into continuous sheets and films of various thicknesses. All, broadly speaking, have plastic use.

RHOMBIC
Referring to crystals having equilateral edges and oblique angles.

RIFFLES
Grooves in a sluice for catching gold in hydraulic mining operations.

S

SACRIFICIAL METAL
The more active of a pair of metals which is oxidized by an electric cell action.

SALTS
Crystalline compounds made up of metals and non-metals. Example: table salt is sodium and chlorine.

SAPONIFICATION
The process of making soap by adding lye to a glyceryl ester.

SARAN
One of the synthetic fibers.

SATURATED SOLUTION
A solution in which the solute in solution is in equilibrium with undissolved solute.

SEDIMENTARY
A term applied to rocks formed from sediment that has been deposited in layers.

SHELL-FILLER
An explosive that requires a severe shock to set it off.

SHERARDIZING
Coating with zinc by allowing zinc vapor to condense on the object.

SILICONES
Unique new group of polymers made by molecular combination of the inorganic chemical, silicone dioxide, with organic chemicals. Produced in variety of forms including silicone fluids, resins and rubber. Silicones have special properties, such as water-repellensy, wide temperature resistance, durability and dielectric property

SILT
A soil which is coarser than clay but finer than sand.

SINGLE REPLACEMENT REACTION
One in which an element replaces another in a compound.

SINTERING
Heating until fusion just begins.

SLAG
A by-product of smelting. It is formed by the action of low melting material (flux) on impurities in the ore. Slags contain calcium and aluminum silicates.

SLAKED LIME
Calcium hydroxide, or calcium oxide, that has united with water.

SMOKELESS POWDER
A nitrocellulose explosive.

SOAP
The sodium or potassium salts of a fatty acid, e.g., $NaC_{18}H_{35}O_2$.

SOLDER
An easily melted alloy, especially one of tin and lead.

SOLUBILITY PRODUCT CONSTANT

The product of the concentrations of the ions of slightly soluble salt at saturation.

SOLUTION

Mixture in which the identities of components are lost as such.

SOLVENT

A substance, usually an organic compound, which dissolves another substance.

SPECIFIC GRAVITY (GASES)

The ratio of the weight of one liter of air to the weight of one liter of the gas.

SPECIFIC GRAVITY (SOLID OR LIQUID)

The ratio of the weight of a unit volume of a substance to the weight of the same volume of water.

SPECIFIC HEAT

The heat required to raise the temperature of one gram of a substance one degree centigrade.

SPECIFIC VOLUME

The volume of one gram of a substance.

SPINNERETS

Thimble-like plates with tiny holes for extruding synthetic fibers.

STALACTITES

Icicle-like masses of calcium carbonate hanging from the roof of limestone caves.

STALAGMITES

Masses of calcium carbonate rising from the floor of limestone caves, formed by dripping of calcium bicarbonate solution from the cave roof.

STANDARD CONDITIONS

$0°$ C. and 1 atmosphere pressure (760 mm.).

STANDARD PRESSURE

A pressure equal to that furnished by a column of mercury 760 mm. high.

STANDARD TEMPERATURE

Zero degrees Centigrade.

STERLING

Containing 92.5% silver, or 925 fine.

S.T.P.

Abbreviation for "standard temperature and pressure."

STRONG ACID

One which is completely ionized in water solutions.

STRONG ELECTROLYTE

One which is ionized almost completely.

STRUCTURE FORMULAS

Formulas that tell how the atoms are joined in the molecules.

SUBLIMATION

A process in which a solid is vaporized and condensed to a solid without passing through the liquid state.

SUPERHEATED WATER

Water heated under pressure to a temperature above the normal boiling point.

SUPERPHOSPHATE

Phosphorus-bearing material made by action or sulfuric acid on phosphate rock to make phosphorus available as a plant nutrient. Phosphorus in soluble form is one of the three essential plant nutrients. (Other two: nitrogen, potassium.)

SUPERSATURATED

Pertaining to a solution saturated at a high temperature which retains the solute in solution as it cools.

SURFACE-ACTIVE AGENT
Any of a group of compounds added to a liquid to modify surface or interface tension. In the case of synthetic detergents, best known surface-active agent, reduction of tension provides cleansing action. Term also includes dispersing, emulsifying, foaming, penetrating and wetting agents. Usually synthetic organic in origin.

SURFACE COATINGS
Term used to cover paint, lacquer, varnish and other chemical compositions used for protecting and/or decorating surfaces.

SURFACTANT
A coined word which means "surface-active agent."

SYNCHROTRON
One of the "atom-smashing" machines for bombarding atomic nuclei.

SYNERGIST
A material which, in combination with another, improves the effectiveness of the combination to a degree in excess of the sum of the effects of the two materials taken independently.

SYNTHESIS
The reaction, or series of reactions, by which a complex compound is obtained from simpler compounds or elements.

SYNTHETIC DETERGENTS
Chemically-tailored cleaning agents soluble in water. Originally developed as soap substitute. Because they do not form insoluble precipitates, they are especially valuable in hard water. See SURFACE-ACTIVE AGENT.

SYNTHETIC RUBBER
Nab-made polymeric chemical with rubber-like attributes. Various types with varying composition and properties. Major types designated as S-type, butyl, neoprene (chloroprene polymers), and N-type.

T

TALL OIL
(Name derived from Swedish TALLOLJA; material first investigated in Sweden-not synonymous with our pine oil.)

Natural mixture of rosin acids, fatty acids, sterols, high molecular weight alcohols and other materials, derived primarily from waste liquors of wood pulp manufacture. Dark brown, viscous, oily liquid often called liquid rosin. Recent encyclopedia lists 38 major industry uses.

TANKAGE
A fertilizer made from slaughter house scraps.

TAR CRUDE
Basic organic raw material derived from distillation of coal tar and used for chemical manufacture.

TEMPERING
Regulation of the iron carbide, and thus the hardness of a piece of steel, by heating and sudden cooling.

TERNARY
Composed of three elements.

TERNE PLATE
Sheet iron coated with an alloy of tin and lead.

THERMITE REACTION
The replacement reaction between a metal, such as aluminum, and an oxide, such as ferric oxide, which liberates much heat.

THERMOPLASTIC TYPE OF PLASTICS
Those that can repeatedly melt or soften with heat and harden on cooling. Examples: vinyls, acrylics, polyethylene.

THERMOSETTING TYPE OF PLASTICS
Those that are heat-set in their final processing to a permanently hard state. Examples: phenolics, ureas and melamines.

THINNER
A liquid, such as turpentine, used in paint to make it spread more easily and penetrate better

TINCTURE
A solution the solvent of which is alcohol, e.g., tincture of iodine.

TITRATION
Determination of the concentration of a solution by comparing it with a standard solution, usually employing burettes for the operation.

TOLUENE ($CH_3C_6H_5$)
Hydrocarbon derived mainly from petroleum but also from coal. Base for TNT, lacquers, saccharin and many other chemicals.

TRIADS
Group of three elements in the same vertical column of the periodic table.

TRIBASIC ACID
An acid containing three replaceable hydrogen atoms per molecule.

TRIPLE SUPERPHOSPHATE
Phosphorus fertilizer of higher phosphorus content than in superphosphate; produced by addition of phosphoric acid to phosphate rock.

TUYERES
The nozzles of the blowpipes of a blast furnace.

TYNDALL EFFECT
The dispersion of a beam of light as it passes through a colloidal solution.

U

ULTRAVIOLET RAYS
Invisible radiations having a shorter wave length than violet light.

UNSLAKED LIME
Calcium oxide, or line to which water has not been added.

U.S.P.
Abbreviation for <u>United States Pharmacopoeia,</u> an official book that specifies strengths and degrees of purity of official remedies.

V

VALENCE
The number of electrons gained, lost, or shared in forming a chemical bond.

VALENCE ELECTRONS
Electrons in the outermost orbit which may be gained or lost in chemical reactions.

VAPOR
A gas that can be converted into a liquid at that temperature by pressure alone.

VAPOR DENSITY
The ratio of the weight of a gas to the weight of an equal volume of hydrogen measured under the same conditions.

VAPOR PRESSURE
The (partial) pressure exerted by a vapor.

VAPOR TENSION
The pressure which a vapor exerts on a liquid when the liquid and vapor are in equilibrium at a given temperature (the maximum vapor pressure for the given temperature).

VAT DYES
Water-insoluble, complex coal tar dyes that can be chemically reduced in a heated solution to a soluble form that will impregnate fibers. Subsequent oxidation then produces insoluble colored dye-stuff remarkably fast to washing, light and chemicals.

VEHICLE
The liquid portion of paint, such as linseed oil, used to hold the paint base in suspension.

VERMICULITE
Mica that has bean expanded with steam to make a light, porous material.

VISCOSITY
(1) The resistance to flow of a liquid.
(2) The internal friction of a liquid.

VITRIFIED
Heated to the point where melting just begins, thus closing pores.

VITRIOL
An acid substance.

VOLUME-VOLUME PROBLEMS
Those in which a known volume of one material is given and the volume of another material involved in the reaction is sought.

VOLT
The electrical pressure required to make a current of one ampere through a resistance of one ohm.

VULCANIZATION
Process of combining rubber (natural, synthetic, or latex) with sulfur and various other additives usually under heat and pressure, in order to eliminate tackiness when warm and brittleness when cool, and to change permanently the material from a thermoplastic to a thermosetting composition. Finally to otherwise improve strength, elasticity, and abrasive resistance.

<u>W</u>

WARFARIN
A new kind of rat poison.

WATER GAS
A fuel gas made by blowing a bast of steam through a bed of red-hot coke.

WATER GLASS
A syrupy solution of sodium silicate.

WATER OF HYDRATION
Water that has united with some chemicals as they form crystals called hydrates.

WEAK ACID
An acid which is but slightly ionized in water solutions.

WEAK ELECTROLYTE
One that is but slightly ionized.

WEIGHTED SILK
Silk that has been dipped in solutions of certain tin salts.

WEIGHT-WEIGHT PROBLEMS
Those in which a known quantity of one material is given and the amount of another material involved in the reaction is sought.

WEIGHT-VOLUME PROBLEMS
Those in which the weight or volume of one material is given and either the weight or volume of another material involved in the reaction is sought

WETTING AGENTS
Materials that reduce the surface tension of a liquid, causing it to spread out better.

X

X-RAYS
Light radiations of high frequency and very short wave length.

Z.

ZEOLITES
Naturally occurring minerals, such as an aluminate of either sodium or potassium.

ZIRCONIUM
A metallic element with an exceedingly high melting point.

CHEMICAL LAWS

1. **AVOGADRO'S HYPOTHESIS**

Equal volumes of gases, under the same conditions of temperature and pressure, contain the same number of molecules.

A liter of oxygen contains the same number of molecules as a liter of hydrogen measured under the same conditions of temperature and pressure.

2. **BOYLE'S LAW**

If the temperature remains constant, the volume of a given mass of gas is inversely proportional to the pressure.

$$\frac{V_1}{V_2} = \frac{P_2}{P_1}$$

Example: If the pressure on a gas is doubled and the temperature is constant, the new volume is one-half the original volume.

3. **CHARLES' LAW**

If the pressure remains constant, the volume of a gas caries directly with the Absolute temperature.

$$\frac{V_1}{V_2} \quad \frac{T_1}{T_2}$$

Example: If the Absolute temperature of a gas is doubled, the volume is also doubled.

4. **GAY-LUSSAC'S LAW OF COMBINING VOLUMES OF GASES**

   The relative combining volumes of gases and their products, if gaseous, may be expressed by small whole numbers.

   Example: One volume of chlorine combines with one volume of hydrogen forming two volumes of hydrogen chloride.

5. **HENRY'S LAW OF GAS SOLUBILITY**

   If the temperature is held constant, the weight of a gas which dissolves in a given volume is proportional to the pressure.

   Example: The greater the pressure, the larger the volume of gas which can be dissolved. Suppose that one liter of water can dissolve 2 grams of carbon dioxide at 1 atmosphere of pressure. If the temperature remains the same, 4 grams can be dissolved if the pressure is increased to 2 atmospheres.

6. **LAW OF CONSERVATION OF ENERGY**

   Energy can neither be created nor destroyed; it may, however, be changed from one form to another.

Example: When coal is burned, stored chemical energy is converted and released as heat energy.

7. LAW OF CONSERVATION OF MATTER (MASS)
Matter can neither be created nor destroyed. If the matter is changed from one form to another, the new products produced have the same mass as the original substances.

8. LAW OF MASS ENERGY
This law expresses the equivalence of mass and energy. It states that energy (E) is equal to mass (m) times the square of the velocity of light (c) in centimeters per second.

$$E = mc^2$$

9. LAW OF DEFINITE PROPORTIONS
Every chemical compound has a definite composition of weight.

Example: If pure water is analyzed its composition will never vary.

There will always be eight times as much oxygen by weight as hydrogen.

10. LAW OF MASS ACTION
The speed of a chemical reaction is proportional to the product of the molecular concentration of the reacting substances.

Example: Mass action refers to the changing of the equilibrium of a reaction by varying the concentration of one or more of the reactants. Thus, the law states that in a reversible reaction the speed at which it occurs depends on the concentration of the reactants.

11. LAW OF MULTIPLE PROPORTIONS
When two elements unite to form more than one compound, the weights of one element which combine with a fixed weight of the other are in the ratio of small whole numbers.

Example: In the compound carbon monoxide (CO), there are 12 grams of carbon and 16 grams of oxygen. In the compound carbon dioxide (CO_2), there are 12 grams of carbon and 16 grams of oxygen. Therefore,

$$\frac{\text{weight of oxygen in CO}}{\text{weight of oxygen in CO}_2} = \frac{1}{2}$$

12. LE CHATELIER'S PRINCIPLE
If a system which is in equilibrium is affected by a change in temperature or pressure, it will adjust itself so that the effect of the change will be reduced to a minimum.

Example: If the pressure on a system in equilibrium is increased, the system will adjust itself so that it will occupy less volume.

13. PERIODIC LAW (MOSELEY'S)
The chemical properties of the elements are a periodic function of their atomic numbers.

GLOSSARY OF COMMON SUBSTANCE

A

COMMON NAME	CHEMICAL NAME	FORMULA
Alum	Potassium aluminum sulfate	$K_2SO_4 \cdot Al_2(SO_4)_3 \cdot 24H_2O$
Alumina	Aluminum oxide	Al_2O_3
Alundum	Fused aluminum oxide	Al_2O_3
Ammonia water	Ammonium hydroxide	NH_4OH
Aniline	Phenyl amine	$C_6H_5NH_2$
Aqua ammonia	A solution of NH_3 in H_2O	NH_4OH
Aqua fortis	Nitric acid	HNO_3
Aqua regia	Hydrochloric and nitric acids	$3 HCl + HNO_3$
Asbestos (principal form)	Hydrated magnesium silicate	$3 MgO \cdot 2 SiO_2 \cdot 2H_2O$
Aspirin	Acetylsalicylic acid	$C_6H_4(COOH)OCOCH_3$

B

Babbitt	Alloy of Sn, Sb, and Cu	
Bakelite	Resin from phenol and formaldehyde	
Baking powder	A mixture of $NaHCO_3$, an acid ingredient, and starch	
Baking soda	Sodium bicarbonate	NaHCO
Bauxite	Hydrated aluminum oxide	$Al_2O_3 \cdot 3H_2O$ and $Al_2O_3 \cdot H_2O$
Bleaching powder	Calcium oxychloride	$CaOCl_2$
Blue vitriol	Cupric sulfate	$CuSO_4$
Bluestone	Cupric sulfate	$CuSO_4$
Bone ash	Calcium phosphate (impure)	$Ca_3(PO_4)_2$
Bone black	Animal charcoal	C
Boracic acid	Boric acid	H_3BO_3
Borax	Sodium tetraborate	$Na_2B_4O_7 \cdot 10 H_2O$
Brass	Alloy of Cu and Zn	
Brimstone	Volcanic sulfur	Impure S
Brine	Sodium chloride solution	NaCl and H_2O
Bronze	Alloy of Cu, Sn, and Zn	

C

Cadium yellow	Cadmium sulfide	CdS
Calcite	Calcium carbonate	$CaCO_3$
Calich	Sodium nitrate (impure)	$NaNO_3$
Calomel	Mercurous chloride	HgCl
Camphor, artificial	Pinene chloride	$C_{10}H_{17}Cl$
Cane sugar	Sucrose	$C_{12}H_{22}O_{11}$
Carbolic acid	Phenol	C_6H_5OH
Carbonic acid gas	Carbon dioxide	CO_2

GLOSSARY OF COMMON SUBSTANCES (CONT'D)

COMMON NAME	CHEMICAL NAME	FORMULA
Caustic potash	Potassium hydroxide	KOH
Caustic soda	Sodium hydroxide	$NaOH$
Ceruse	Basic lead carbonate	$2\ PbCO_3 \cdot Pb(OH)_2$
Chalk	Calcium carbonate (impure)	$CaCO_3$
Chile saltpeter	Sodium nitrate (impure)	$NaNO_3$
China clay	Aluminum silicate	$Al_2O_3 \cdot 2SiO_2 \cdot 2H_2O$
Chloride of lime	Calcium oxychloride	$CaOCl_2$
Chrome alum	Potassium chromium sulfate	$K_2SO_4 \cdot Cr_2(SO_4)_3 \cdot 24\ H_2O$
Cinnabar	Mercuric sulfide	HgS
Coke	Carbon (impure)	C
Common salt	Sodium chloride	$NaCl$
Copperas	Ferrous sulfate	$FeSO_4 \cdot 7H_2O$
Corrosive sublimate	Mercuric chloride	$HgCl_2$
Corundum	Aluminum oxide	Al_2O_3
Cream of tartar	Potassium hydrogen tartrate	$KHC_4H_4O_6$

D

Dextrose	Glucose	$C_6H_{12}O_6$
Diamond	Carbon	C
Dry ice	Solid carbon dioxide	CO_2

E

Epsom salts	Magnesium sulfate	$MgSO_4$

F

Feldspar (one form)	Potassium aluminum silicate	$KAlSi_3O_8$
Firedamp	Methane	CH_4
Flowers of sulfur	Sulfur	S
Fluorspar	Calcium fluoride	CaF_2
Fool's gold	Iron pyrite	FeS_2

G

Galena	Lead sulfide	PbS
Glass	A solid solution containing a mixture of silicates	
Glauber's salt	Sodium sulfate	$Na_2SO_4 \cdot 10H_2O$
Glucose	Dextrose	$C_6H_{12}O_6$
Glycerin	Glycerol	$C_3H_5(OH)_3$
Grain alcohol	Ethyl alcohol	C_2H_5OH
Graphite	Carbon	C
Green vitriol	Ferrous sulfate	$FeSO_4$
Gypsum	Calcium sulfate	$CaSO_4 \cdot 2H_2O$

H

Horn silver	Silver chloride	$AgCl$
Household ammonia	Ammonium hydroxide	NH_4OH
Hypo	Sodium thiosulfate	$Na_2S_2O_3 \cdot 5H_2O$

GLOSSARY OF COMMON SUBSTANCES (CONT'D)

COMMON NAME	CHEMICAL NAME	FORMULA
K		
Kaolin	Hydrogen aluminum silicate	$H_2Al_2(SiO_4)_2 \cdot H_2O$
L		
Lampblack	Carbon (impure)	C
Lanolin	Cholesterol	$C_{27}H_{46}O$
Laughing gas	Nitrous oxide	N_2O
Levulose	Fructose	$C_6H_{12}O_6$
Lime, hydra ted	Calcium hydroxide	$Ca(OH)_2$
Lime, quick	Calcium oxide	CaO
Lime, slaked	Calcium hydroxide	$Ca(OH)_2$
Limestone	Calcium carbonate	$CaCO_3$
Limewater	Calcium hydroxide solution	$Ca(OH)_2$
Litharge	Lead oxide	PbO
Lithopone	Zinc sulfide and barium sulfate	ZnS and $BaSO_4$
Lunar caustic	Silver nitrate	$AgNO_3$
Lye	Sodium hydroxide	NaOH
Magnesia	Magnesium oxide	MgO
Magnesite	Magnesium carbonate	$MgCO_3$
Malachite	Basic copper carbonate	$CuCo_3 \cdot Cu(OH)_2$
Marble	Calcium carbonate (impure)	$CaCO_3$
Marsh gas	Methane	CH_4
Methanol	Methyl alcohol	CH_3OH
Minium	Lead tetroxide	Pb_3O_4
Moth balls	Naphthalene	$C_{10}H_8$
Muriate of potash	Potassium chloride	KCl
Muriatic acid	Hydrochloric acid	HCl
N		
Niter	Potassium nitrate	KNO_3
O		
Oil of bitter almonds	Benzaldehyde	C_6H_5CHO
Oil of vitriol	Sulfuric acid	H_3SO_4
Oil of wintergreen	Methyl salicylate	$CH_3COOC_6H_4OH$
Oileum	Fuming sulfuric acid	$H_2SO_4 \cdot SO_3$
P		
Pearl	Calcium carbonate	$CaCO_3$
Phosgene	Carbonyl chloride	$COCl_2$
Plaster of Paris	Calcium sulfate	$2CaSO_4 \cdot H_2O$
Potash	Potassium carbonate or potassiuin hydroxide	K_2CO_3 or KOH
Pyrolusite	Manganese dioxide	MnO_2
Q		
Quicklime	Calcium oxide	CaO
Quicksilver	Mercury	Hg

GLOSSARY OF COMMON SUBSTANCES (CONT'D)

COMMON NAME	CHEMICAL NAME	FORMULA
R		
Rochelle salt	Potassium sodium tartrate	$KNaC_4H_4O_6$
Route	Ferric oxide	Fe_2O_3
S		
Sal ammoniac	Ammonium chloride	NH_4Cl
Sal soda	Sodium carbonate	Na_2CO_3
Salt of sorrell	Potassium acid oxalate	$KHC_2O_4 \cdot H_2O$
Saltpeter	Sodium nitrate	$NaNO_3$
Sand	Silicon dioxide	SiO_2
Silica	Silicon dioxide	SiO_2
Slaked lime	Calcium hydroxide	$Ca(OH)_2$
Soda lime	Calcium oxide & sodium hydroxide	CaO and $NaOH$
Soap (one kind)	Sodium stearate	$C_{17}H_{35}COONa$
Spirit of hartshorn	Ammonium hydroxide	NH_4OH
Spirit of wine	Ethyl alcohol	C_2H_5OH
Sugar	Sucrose	$C_{12}H_{22}O_{11}$
Sugar of lead	Lead acetate	$Pb(C_2H_3O_2)$
Superphosphate	Calcium sulfate & calcium acid phosphate	$CaSO_4$ and $Ca(H_2PO_4)_2$
T		
TABLE SALT	Sodium chloride	$NaCl$
TALC	Hydrated magnesium silicate	$3\,MgO \cdot 4SiO_2 \cdot H_2O$
TARTAR EMETIC	Potassium antimonyl tartrate	$2\,K(SbO)C_4H_4O_6 \cdot H_2O$
V		
Vinegar	Acetic acid, dilute	$HC_2H_3O_2$
W		
Water glass	Sodium silicate	Na_2SiO_3
White lead	Basic lead carbonate	$2PbCO_3 \cdot Pb(OH)_2$
White vitriol	Zinc sulfate	$ZnSO_4$
Whiting	Calcium carbonate	$CaCO_3$
Wood alcohol	Methyl alcohol	CH_3OH
Z		
Zinc blende	Zinc sulfide	ZnS
Zinc white	Zinc oxide	ZnO

CHEMICAL ELEMENTS AND SYMBOLS

NAME OF ELEMENT	SYMBOL	ATOMIC NUMBER	ATOMIC WEIGHT
		A	
Actinium	AC	89	227.0
Aluminum	Al	13	26.98
Americium	Am	95	[243]
Antimony	Sb	51	121.76
Argon	A	18	39.944
Arsenic	As	33	74.91
Astatine	At	85	[210]
		B	
Barium	Ba	56	137.36
Berkelium	Bk	97	[245]
Beryllium	Be	4	9.013
Bismuth	Bi	83	209.00
Boron	B	5	10.82
Bromine	Br	35	79.916
		C	
Cadmium	Cd	48	112.41
Calcium	Ca	20	40.08
Californium	Cf	98	[246]
Carbon	c	6	12.011
Cerium	Cc	58	140.13
Cesium	Cs	55	132.91
Chlorine	Cl	17	35.457
Chromium	Cr	24	52.01
Cobalt	Co	27	58.94
Copper	Cu	29	63.54
Curium	Cm	96	[243]
		D	
Dysprosium	Dy	66	162.46
		E	
Erbium	Er	68	167.2
Europium	Eu	63	152.0
		F	
Fluorine	F	9	19.00
Francium	Fr	87	[223]
		G	
Gadolinium	Gd	64	156.9
Gallium	Ga	31	69.72
Germanium	Ge	32	72.60
Gold	Au	79	197.0
		H	
Hafnium	Hf	72	178.6
Helium	He	2	4.003
Holmium	Ho	67	164.94
Hydrogen	H	1	1.0080
		I	
Indium	In	49	114.76
Iodine	I	53	126.91
Iridium	Ir	77	192.2
Iron	Fe	26	55.85
		K	
Krypton	Kr	36	83.80
		L	
Lanthanum	La	57	138.92

CHEMICAL ELEMENTS AND SYMBOLS (CONT'D)

NAME OF ELEMENT	SYMBOL	ATOMIC NUMBER	ATOMIC WEIGHT
Lead	Pb	82	207.21
Lithium	Li	3	6.940
Lutetium	Lu	71	174.99
M			
Magnesium	Mg	12	24.32
Manganese	Mn	25	54.94
Mercury	Hg	80	200.61
Molybdenum	Mo	42	95.95
N			
Neodymium	Nd	60	144.27
Neon	Ne	10	20.183
Neptunium	Np	93	[2373]
Nickel	Ni	28	58.69
Niobium	Nb	41	92.91
Nitrogen	N	7	14.008
O			
Osmium	Os	76	190.2
Oxygen	O	8	16.0000
P			
Palladium	Pd	46	106.7
Phosphorus	P	15	30.975
Platinum	Pt	78	195.23
Plutonium	Pu	94	[242]
Polonium	Po	84	210.0
Potassium	K	19	39.100
Praseodymium	Pr	59	140.92
Promethium	Pm	61	[145]
Protactinium	Pa	91	231.
R			
Radium	Ra	88	226.05
Radon	Rn	86	222.
Rhenium	Re	75	186.31
Rhodium	Rh	45	102.91
Rubidium	Rb	37	85.48
Ruthenium	Ru	44	101.1
S			
Samarium	Sm	62	150.43
Scandium	Sc	21	44.96
Selenium	Se	34	78.96
Silicon	Si	14	28.09
Silver	Ag	47	107.880
Sodium	Na	11	22.991
Strontium	Sr	38	87.63
Sulfur	S	16	32.066
T			
Tantalum	Ta	73	180.95
Technetium	Tc	43	[99]
Tellurium	Te	52	127.61
Terbium	Tb	65	158.93
Thallium	Tl	81	204.39
Thor ium	Th	90	232.05
Thulium	Tm	69	168.94
Tin	Sn	50	118.70
Titanium	Ti	22	47.90
Tungsten	W	74	183.92

		U	
Uranium	U	92	238.07
		V	
Vanadium	V	23	50.95
		X	
Xenon	Xe	54	131.3
		Y	
Ytterbium	Yb	70	173.04
Yttrium	Y	39	88.92
		Z	
Zinc	Zn	30	65.38
Zirconium	Zr	40	91.22

(NOTE: Brackets indicate the isotope of longest known half-life.)

PERIODIC TABLE OF THE ELEMENTS

IA	IIA	IIIB	IVB	VB	VIB	VIIB	VIIIB			IB	IIB	IIIA	IVA	VA	VIA	VIIA	Noble gases
1 H 1.008																	2 He 4.003
3 Li 6.941	4 Be 9.012											5 B 10.81	6 C 12.011	7 N 14.007	8 O 15.999	9 F 18.998	10 Ne 20.179
11 Na 22.990	12 Mg 24.305											13 Al 26.982	14 Si 28.086	15 P 30.974	16 S 32.06	17 Cl 35.453	18 Ar 39.948
19 K 39.102	20 Ca 40.08	21 Sc 44.956	22 Ti 47.90	23 V 50.941	24 Cr 51.996	25 Mn 54.938	26 Fe 55.847	27 Co 58.933	28 Ni 58.71	29 Cu 63.546	30 Zn 65.37	31 Ga 69.72	32 Ge 72.59	33 As 74.922	34 Se 78.96	35 Br 79.904	36 Kr 83.80
37 Rb 85.468	38 Sr 87.62	39 Y 88.906	40 Zr 91.22	41 Nb 92.906	42 Mo 95.94	43 Tc 98.602	44 Ru 101.07	45 Rh 102.905	46 Pd 106.4	47 Ag 107.868	48 Cd 112.40	49 In 114.82	50 Sn 118.69	51 Sb 121.75	52 Te 127.60	53 I 126.905	54 Xe 131.30
55 Cs 132.905	56 Ba 137.34	57 La 138.905	72 Hf 178.49	73 Ta 180.948	74 W 183.85	75 Re 186.2	76 Os 190.2	77 Ir 192.22	78 Pt 195.09	79 Au 196.966	80 Hg 200.59	81 Tl 204.37	82 Pb 207.19	83 Bi 208.2	84 Po (~210)	85 At ~210	86 Rn (~222)
87 Fr (223)	88 Ra 226.02	89 Ac (227)	104	105													

58 Ce 140.12	59 Pr 140.907	60 Nd 144.24	61 Pm (145)	62 Sm 150.4	63 Eu 151.96	64 Gd 157.25	65 Tb 158.925	66 Dy 162.50	67 Ho 154.930	68 Er 167.26	69 Tm 168.934	70 Yb 173.04	71 Lu 174.97
90 Th 232.038	91 Pa 231.036	92 U 238.029	93 Np 237.048	94 Pu (244)	95 Am (243)	96 Cm (247)	97 Bk (247)	98 Cf (251)	99 Es (254)	100 Fm (257)	101 Md (256)	102 No (254)	103 Lr (257)

www.ingramcontent.com/pod-product-compliance
Lightning Source LLC
Chambersburg PA
CBHW082207300426
44117CB00016B/2708